Building Library 3.0

CHANDOS
INFORMATION PROFESSIONAL SERIES

Series Editor: Ruth Rikowski
(email: Rikowskigr@aol.com)

Chandos' new series of books are aimed at the busy information professional. They have been specially commissioned to provide the reader with an authoritative view of current thinking. They are designed to provide easy-to-read and (most importantly) practical coverage of topics that are of interest to librarians and other information professionals. If you would like a full listing of current and forthcoming titles, please visit our website www.chandospublishing.com or email info@chandospublishing.com or telephone +44 (0) 1223 891358.

New authors: we are always pleased to receive ideas for new titles; if you would like to write a book for Chandos, please contact Dr Glyn Jones on email gjones@chandospublishing.com or telephone number +44 (0) 1993 848726.

Bulk orders: some organisations buy a number of copies of our books. If you are interested in doing this, we would be pleased to discuss a discount. Please email info@chandospublishing.com or telephone +44(0) 1223 891358.

Building Library 3.0

Issues in creating a culture of participation

WOODY EVANS

Chandos Publishing

Oxford • Cambridge • New Delhi

Chandos Publishing
TBAC Business Centre
Avenue 4
Station Lane
Witney
Oxford OX28 4BN
UK
Tel: +44 (0) 1993 848726
Email: info@chandospublishing.com
www.chandospublishing.com

Chandos Publishing is an imprint of Woodhead Publishing Limited

Woodhead Publishing Limited
Abington Hall
Granta Park
Great Abington
Cambridge CB21 6AH
UK
www.woodheadpublishing.com

First published in 2009

ISBN:
978 1 84334 497 1

British Library Cataloguing-in-Publication Data.
A catalogue record for this book is available from the British Library.

Typeset by Domex e-Data Pvt. Ltd.
Printed in the UK and USA.

Printed in the UK by 4edge Limited - www.4edge.co.uk

To the memory of Durwood Williams, and with hope
for Griffin Evans.

Contents

List of abbreviations

AIM	AOL Instant Messenger
ALA	American Library Association
CIPA	Children's Internet Protection Act
COI	community of interest
COPPA	Children's Online Privacy Protection Act
DDMS	Department of Defense Metadata Specification
FRBR	functional requirements for bibliographic records
ILL	inter-library lending
ILS	integrated library system
MARC	Machine-Readable Cataloguing
MMOG	massively multiplayer online game
MMORPG	massively multiplayer online role-playing game
MPAA	Motion Picture Association of America
MUD	multi-user dungeon
MUFON	Mutual UFO Network
NMC	New Media Consortium
NOAA	National Oceanic and Atmospheric Administration
OCLC	Online Computer Library Center
OPAC	online public access catalogue
RDA	resource description and access
RDF	resource description framework
RFID	radio frequency identification

RIAA   Recording Industry Association of
                America
STAR-TIDES   Sustainable Technologies, Accelerated
                Research – Transportable Infrastructures
                for Development and Emergency Support
XML   eXtensible Markup Language

List of figures

Acknowledgements

Thanks are due to more folks than I could mention, but I must especially thank the following for shaping me as a librarian or as a writer. Thanks to Derek Reece, Jo Klemm, Mark D'Olive, and Andrew Strohschein for thinking hard and talking hard so often about libraries and their future. Thanks to Joseph Mehl for arguing for a better world, and working for one. Thanks to Deb Liptak for the smarts, generosity, and for encouraging me to query Barbara Quint (thanks to bq for being a really great editor). Thanks to Steven Barthelme for letting me in on so many writing workshops, and for being tough with me. Thanks to Andrew Albanese. Thanks to the anthropology and library science departments at the University of Southern Mississippi – especially to James Flanagan and Teresa Welsh. Thanks to the librarians of Tarrant County College, Air Combat Command, and of Hattiesburg's public library. Thanks to my family and friends, my parents Kenny Evans and Sherry Huckeby, my sister April Ralston, my uncle Steven Markley, and my grandfather, Robert Evans. Thanks to my brother, Jared Hegwood.

Thanks to my wife, Aubree Evans, for the faith.

Thanks to all those librarians who stink like the black dregs of burnt coffee pots and tobacco smoke, lapels stained with Red Bull and baby spit-up, who come to work hungry to serve the common good, zealous about getting the information to the people – to the librarians, the library staff, who *believe* in it, who pour their *hearts* into it. Who *fight* for it.

Introduction

Since you're reading this text, you have probably noticed that libraries are in the midst of a profound transformation. This transformation has been dosed with octane since the advent of the information revolution, and since the personal computer, and since digital databases. Now, twenty and thirty years on, collaborative and user-produced content on the Web is taking the changes even further. The transformation is spilling out in front of us much more quickly than we can move to catch up with it.

Some libraries would rather start marching toward the cliffs, denying the cues from their users; and if enough information professionals follow that path, libraries the world over are headed for woeful troubles indeed. But there is plenty of hope in this time of ferment, and a hefty number of libraries have been working close to the roots of their communities, serving patrons where they live and how they live. This tendency, acted upon with skill and vision, can see us through these times of continuing confusion. Libraries looking to survive into the twenty-second century are putting their users first. These libraries are embracing the ethos of 'Library 2.0' and are modifying the tools of Web 2.0 to ensure their relevance in the coming world of Web 3.0.

This book is for information professionals and librarians who want to reach out to their users with the tools of Web 2.0 wisely. It is for librarians who want new ways of reaching their users and who dream of building communities around their collections despite limitations in collection size, library location, or money. Being, too, for the librarian who lacks the funding to buy her way into advanced services, the tools we explore will often err toward the cheap or free: whether in Mize, Mississippi or Catandica, Mozambique, this is for the librarian who needs to *get the information to the people*. And here we show her how – with tools that can be used in many languages and with diverse softwares and platforms. The major theme of this book is the importance of the social considerations of our new information tools; its thesis is:

> Libraries using Web 2.0 tools are going to get a lot closer to their communities. Doing so is not easy, and takes you deeper into participation with your patrons than you may have yet been willing to go; all of this prepares you for librarianship in the world of the semantic web.

This book is, on the surface, about technology and about using new technological tools to connect libraries with library users. Digging deeper, though, this book (and, indeed, 'Library 2.0') is about a way of serving our communities, reaching library users, and opening up our processes so that our patrons see their own stakes laying in front of them on the circulation desk. To serve our library users we must be sincere, confident, and passionate, and this book *cannot teach you that*. Computers merely aid us. Technology is but a means. If you are passionate about providing information to your community, then keep reading. We've got a lot to explore, so blog your notes and ask plenty of questions (to each other, and, if you like, to me[1]).

Exercise caution, however. We will not be building Library 3.0 just because it's the new or trendy thing to do (indeed, the use of the term 'point-oh' has become, by early 2009, somewhat annoying now); and when we build it, we will build it always with the goal of improving service for our users first and foremost. Too many librarians have made the mistake of leading their libraries into the newest technology in order to seem cool and hip to their early-adopting patrons. We here have different reasons for going deep.

There are three broad sections in this book. The first deals with the concept of the '2.0 library', and the new (post-web browser) library patron. The second considers specific technological applications to benefit library patrons, such as mobile computing tools, social software applications, and radio frequency identification technology. Thirdly, we consider how these advances affect the fundamentals of good information architecture, usability, and findability.

These three points build up to a conclusion that takes us back to our roots – good search practice, good soft skills, critical thinking, and how we must bring these to bear on our patrons' information problems – and prepares us for the kind of library service that might still have impact in a world learning to navigate a semantic web. Throughout, you will find a pointed concern with the way these changes in information technology change the way we must interact with those we serve.

Library 3.0 is the library that is still in existence after the semantic web and the 'internet of things' become common parts of information seeking, resource use, and daily life. That is where we are headed, right now. The hope is that the following text will be a reality check for those of us who want to begin putting the social web to work for our users, and that this text will inspire all of us information professionals to try harder and do more, no matter what level of technology we have access to.

Now let's go.

Note

1. A place to discuss these issues with other librarians will be maintained at: *http://buildingthree.blogspot.com/*.

About the author

Woody Evans is a public services librarian at Tarrant County College in Arlington, Texas. Originally from Southern Mississippi, he first felt the pull to involve himself with libraries when he learned that librarians in the town nearest his swampland home hid books they didn't like (mainly on occult topics) beneath the circulation desk. His ire stirred, he started working in libraries part-time and went on to get his graduate degree in library and information science at the University of Southern Mississippi. He has lived and worked in rural Staffordshire, UK; in Tu'cheng City near Taipei, Taiwan; and in the American West. As a librarian and private researcher, he has worked for military, corporate, and academic organizations. He has become especially interested in the socio-cultural aspects of how people participate in finding, sharing, and using information, and hopes to continue such research in future works. His work can be read in *American Libraries*, *Library Journal*, *Searcher Magazine*, *ONLINE*, *Information Today*, *The Journal of Evolution and Technology*, *H+ Magazine*, *Mississippi Libraries*, *Rain Taxi Review of Books*, and others. He's got a beautiful (and patient) wife, and a brilliant son. This year Woody is finally getting around to reading Shelby Foote.

The author may be contacted at:

http://www.woodyevans.com/

Part 1
Basics

Library 2.0: the fundamentals

This idea of a 'Library 2.0' is recent, and is a simple portmanteau of *library* and *Web 2.0*. The idea is to apply Web 2.0 tools and values to library collections, library catalogs, and library service as a whole. The term 'Library 2.0' was coined by Michael Casey, technology director for a public library in Atlanta, Georgia, United States. Casey first used the term on his blog *LibraryCrunch* to describe a participatory way of doing librarianship with one's library patrons. His post 'Where's MY OPAC Browser?' from September 23, 2005 sums up the inclination to bring integrated library systems, public library websites, and catalogs into the realm of Web 2.0:

> I want to sit down at the OPAC (another word that needs updated) and have it remember me, either through a login or other, simple, method. I want my bookmarks, my saved titles, my search history. I want to be able to write reviews and make suggestions, I want to add friends to my social network and let them see my reviews and what I've liked and disliked. I want a built-in, fully customizable aggregator, a to-do list, a place to take notes and save files, and I want access to this from any computer in the world, not just the one at my library. All this exists, of course, in bits and pieces – all

of it through Web 2.0. Look to Netvibes, Flickr, NetFlix, Backpack, and many other Ajax developments. Is *anyone* listening?

Here we have Web 2.0 notions (a personal, personalized, and interactive web space) applied to the library OPAC (online public access catalog); and here Casey envisions a *smart* OPAC that performs better because it performs socially, giving him the ability to add friends, share reviews, exchange comments about favorite (or despicable) reads. We can imagine him sitting down frustrated over a quick lunch at his desk after dealing with some incompatibility issue between the Opera web browser and his library's online catalog, exasperated that his patrons cannot tag their own books like they can tag pictures in Flickr, and banging out this blog post between bites of steaming microwaved potatoes: 'Is *anyone* listening?' It seemed for a very long time that no librarians were listening, though Yahoo!, Google, Amazon, and the rest were very clearly cashing in on Web 2.0 applications. Library patrons (and bewildered librarians) were left wondering if the library administrators would ever get it.

Web 2.0, a term coined by technology publisher Tim O'Reilly (2005), is a portmanteau of 'World Wide Web' and the common way to designate new versions of software products with a decimal number (such as Microsoft Windows 3.2.1, or Adobe Photoshop Elements 5.0). The term stresses that the most common interface for the Internet, the World Wide Web as represented on web browsers, is in a state of transition from an earlier 'version' to something more advanced. At the core of this advancement is a tilt toward applications that allow for a greater social aspect to web use. Casey and others had imagined a social web presence, a social catalog, for their libraries. Library 2.0 would be a more advanced way to serve patrons, based on better access and customizable views of library holdings.

What is Web 2.0 for?

Web 2.0 has evolved because people wanted to use the Internet to interact with other people. Figure 1.1 shows how the concept is built of many smaller parts and pieces that all get folks further along in the process of connecting with other folks online. Meetup.com, for example, 'helps groups of people with shared interests plan meetings and form offline clubs in local communities around the world' (Meetup Note, 2008). Meetup famously helped fuel interest in Howard Dean's campaign in the 2004 United States Presidential Primaries: his supporters 'met' online and then let their 'meat' meet in bars and libraries and parks offline.

Figure 1.1   Web 2.0 Snapshot of Ideas

Source: Markus Angermeier (*http://upload.wikimedia.org/wikipedia/commons/a/ a7/Web_2.0_Map.svg*).

Blogs: flagship of the social web

Blogging is a great example (perhaps the best example) of Web 2.0, because it is an activity that requires reading and writing on the Web, commenting on other blogs, making use of audio and visual media to express ideas, and the transformation of massive numbers of individual users of the Internet into publishers on the Internet. Let's consider blogging as a 2.0 activity in detail.

To start a blog (and let's take it as a free, web-based blog, on a platform like Blogger or Wordpress), you need an account with the blog hosting service. For a Blogger blog, that means setting up a Google account since Google acquired Blogger in 2004. Google accounts are free, and once your account is created (which it can be, it is worth noting, anonymously), you get access to a wide variety of Google's tools and applications, like the Gmail e-mail accounts, an online document repository and web-based word processor, image and video hosting, etc. The username you set up for a Blogger blog account might be totally different to the one you use for a Wordpress blog, or your LiveJournal pages, so already blogging is edging us into an online world where identity is unfixed (and this will turn out to be an important element in Library 2.0). Setting up a blog on Blogger 'is easy', according to the site, and can be done in only three steps: create an account, create a name for your blog, and choose the template. Wordpress makes it similarly simple to start and maintain a blog by offering a free account, various free blog templates, and social web widgets.

Creating the blog's name is an opportunity for marketing yourself, your library, or a set of services offered at your library. A smartly named blog may tie into a wider effort by an organization to bring a suite of 2.0 services together.

Using your library's name in the blog title is an easy and direct way to brand your blog. Marin County Free Library, of Marin County California, has a blog titled Marin County Free Library Blog (*http://www.marincountyfreelibrary .blogspot.com/*). Don't be quick to disparage a plain-and-simple blog title like this – there is zero ambiguity about who is responsible for the posts or who provides the services described therein. It's very direct: Galway Public Libraries Blog is a blog about services at Galway Public Libraries (*http://galwaylibrary.blogspot.com/*). Easy.

But the potential also exists for viral marketing of library services, for collaborative (multi-library) blogs, and for librarians to blog independently of their libraries or without official sanction (as many librarians have had to do while waiting for administrators to catch up). Of course a multitude of possibilities and varieties exist here, and should be explored and exploited for the benefit of the library patrons whenever possible and practical.

The template choice is largely aesthetic – but it is also, very importantly, an *infosthetic* choice, to borrow from the title of one of my favorite blogs (Andrew Vande Moere's *information aesthetics* site at *http://infosthetics.com/*). The template design is an exercise in information architecture made miniature. Every detail, from the font color to the manner of presentation for the blogroll in the sidebar, impacts the user's experiences. Each choice must be made carefully. Library blogs hosted on blogger might find it useful to echo colors, fonts, and layout schemes from the library's official letterhead, promotional materials, and websites – or to choose opposite color schemes that echo the color relationships but on the other side of the color wheel. A library blog for a manga book club might use colors from Tokyopop's website or corporate logos as a subtle tonal reminder of the blog's aim and content.

Even as we move toward consideration of widgets, sidebar items, and JavaScript gizmos, it pays to remember basic usability concepts and information architecture principles. Though Jakob Nielsen may get taken to task for not addressing aesthetic and psychological responses to information design (Dillon, 2000), his style of usability engineering is rarely dismissed wholesale as a set of bad ideas – the basic tenets he propounds in *Usability Engineering* such as 'good' error messages, logical numbering or other sequential formatting for items on a site, efficiency, consistency, and others, should ever be borne in our minds as we begin our in-depth fiddling with a widgetized web (Nielsen, 1994).

A glance at Nielsen's own useit.com, however, will disabuse you in short order of the idea that any extremely usable site is also a perfectly pretty one; high-contrast is not always a good strategy in information architecture, even if it aids the legally blind. Indeed, in this age of Google Accessible Search and highly customizable browser tools, our aesthetic choices can afford to be more subtle and pleasant without disenabling disabled users from using our sites.

Usability is one of the many subfields within the field of information architecture. Information architecture encompasses so much material that it may be in danger of being regarded as too broad and too general a field to be useful; but like another generalist field of study, anthropology, it can yield extremely specific and actionable analyses. The vague and insterstitial regions of the generalist are places of great fermentation, and, in fact, information architecture has plenty to teach us librarians about aesthetics, organization, design, and usability, because its generalism is balanced by its reliance on detailed knowledge of web design, software engineering, and choice architecture (Morville et al., 2002: 4). We want to make information *findable*, whatever format or context said information may find itself embedded within. Without a searchable or browsable index, we find nothing. Without an aesthetically tolerable search interface, we are not likely to spend much time searching for or finding the information that we need.

Peter Morville, a very able information architect (and leader in the movement for the field's growing recognition), writes about the importance of these elements in reaching a state of findability, which he defines (2005: 4) as: 'a. The quality of being locatable or navigable. b. The degree to which a particular object is easy to discover or locate. c. The degree to which a system or environment supports navigation and retrieval.' Findabilty, though defined here very broadly, applies to pulp paperbacks just as well as it does to comments on a blog posting. Our task is to find ways to integrate all the elements of usability and findability for our patrons' sakes.

Back to blogs. It can be too easy to become distracted by questions of format, and Web 2.0 exacerbates the problem. Even in the 1.0 world of business culture, questions about the 'memo-ness' of e-mails emerged; Morville quotes Crowston and Williams: 'Genre is not identical to the medium of the communication – a memo may be realized on paper or in an electronic mail message, while electronic mail may be used to deliver memos or inquiries' (2005: 145). Exactly so. A web widget may be a medium, a carrier, of information, but the widget is not the genre; a widget may report stock values, or play folk songs. In all media, attention to the issues of usefulness, usability, and findability for our communities must be foremost in our efforts to organize information resources. Organizational cultures had to shift into a new way of thinking about messages with the advent of the Web in the 1990s. Libraries and their librarians would be gravely remiss to misunderstand this basic principle of information science and communication. As Marshall McLuhan said: the medium is not the message. Blogs do of course, as a premier exemplar of 2.0-ness, present a number of interesting questions related to format.

In Blogger, you can add any variety of 'page elements' to the different fields of your template's layout. There are page elements for the sidebar, blog posts, and footer areas.

The brief explanations below each element name listed on the Blogger site provide a basic, official description of the elements function, but some of these elements are wildly expandable. The HTML/JavaScript element allows you to run code independent of Blogger, from other outside applications. This might be code that you have written, or it could be a social network application or live feed from another website.

That's blogs – if you want to see how the web is changing, read lots of blogs on lots of subjects, and less for their content than for the tools they employ to deliver the content.

Web 2.0 in the library

Web 2.0 is an already dated term, but its implications are not yet fully realized, especially for librarianship. Web 2.0 is probably best described by a meme map like that in Figure 1.1, because it's a collection of ideas, rather amorphous, and not yet strict or finite. That is because it is a process, and a self-defining process. That is, guided by broad generalities like 'participatory' and 'dynamic' and 'collaborative,' experimenters on the Web have let their *actions* shape the Web into Web 2.0. Web 2.0 is not something that an online service necessarily endeavors to become; rather, the attributes of the delivery of the online service itself, as it allows greater input and modification from its users, is what incrementally creates and defines Web 2.0.

So, if Web 2.0 has been built by activities, what are the nature of these activities? Three of the overriding themes of Tim O'Reilly's (2005) piece on Web 2.0 are participation, tagging, and syndication.

Participation means that the Internet is no longer a one-way roadway. Users create content and share it with other users, autonomously, independent of corporate sanction, and often anonymously. The Internet provides communication platforms, and the people communicate. Wikis, and the very wide and open suite of MediaWiki tools and platforms like Wikipedia, are a good example of participation in action. Millions of contributors add and edit content to wikis, discuss addition and deletion policies, citation standards, and writing quality, and *collectively* build the biggest encyclopedia on Earth. In the era of Web 1.0, addition of content was largely limited to venues such as online forums and personal home pages.

Tagging is our ability to describe information objects (documents, photos, music files, videos, blog posts) with an informal system of categorization. Tags are just words we use to describe something. A search in Flickr for the term 'blue' returns image results that contributors have described as 'blue', whether or not the image is blue or is formally titled blue, or has the word 'blue' in its file name.

Syndication brings the web to the user. RSS ('really simple syndication') lets a user subscribe to a page written in XML that has changing components, and it organizes and sends the 'news' items to a location convenient for the user. This may be a news aggregator, like Bloglines, a desktop aggregator, or just a web browser.

Interaction and collaboration fueled by a more usable and customizable World Wide Web interface is the version of Web 2.0 which leads us to Library 2.0. Arguments for and against the need for or desirability of Library 2.0 have been made lengthily elsewhere. Library 2.0 is being built in exactly the same way Web 2.0 was. Library 2.0 is not something that an organization or government bureaucracy necessarily endeavors to transform its libraries into; rather, the attributes of the daily delivery of excellent library service itself, as the library works to allow greater input and modification of services from its users, is what incrementally creates Library 2.0.

Let us return to the OPAC. Collections of information need finding aids in order to be useful to information seekers, no doubt, and *the catalog* was the way you found your way through large physical collections. The catalog (or 'card' catalog) was a set of metadata about the books, printed on cardstock in a standardized format, and housed in wooden drawers (see Figure 1.2). The catalog was redundant, which

Figure 1.2   Traditional library card catalog

Source: Marcus Gossler (*http://upload.wikimedia.org/wikipedia/commons/7/7e/ Schlagwortkatalog.jpg*).

was good, making information available in alphabetical order about the *subjects* of the books, the *authors'* names of the books, and the *titles* of the works in the collection. This, in fact, was a limited *faceted* viewing tool for the collection's metadata, giving information seekers the ability to tilt, if you will, the data to one of three angles. This catalog was intensely physical, and the physical loss of a physical card in the catalog was a serious blow to the accessibility of this eminently physical collection. Without these finding aids, these cards in the catalog, library patrons would be almost entirely at the whim of chance in stumbling across useful items in the collection. Indeed, the only thing that might save them from endless stumbling would be an individual librarian's detailed knowledge of his collection.

Yet there was a Library 2.0 element to even the card catalog. Patrons could write notes on the cards. This marginalia of metadata could help other information seekers by providing suggestions, shortcuts, and other brief notes about the usefulness of the books. Libraries, overwhelmingly, found such notes a good reason to retype the card. The catalog must be kept pristine, tidy, orderly, and uniquely under the control of the professionals. This quiet (subversive, perhaps) attempt at 2.0 was unsanctioned, grassroots, intermittent, and incoherent. It would take decades and much digitization before the organization itself and the library users found synergy in this regard. There is, of course, still resistance from the professionals about allowing the patrons to write in the catalog.

Digitization of this catalog data was a greatly beneficial step in ensuring the findability of books. The existence and condition of the catalog was no longer bound to mere physical circumstances of paper cards, though it was now fully bound to power outages, electromagnetic disturbances, and the human error that is so greatly magnified by the click of a keyboard (*whoops, didn't mean to delete that whole directory!*). The *integrated library system* provided access to library intranets, for catalog searching and browsing, account services like book requests and renewals, and, later, even connection to the Internet with basic web browsers like Lynx. As the World Wide Web grew and developed, so did these library management systems, and so did the OPAC.

OPACs are still overwhelmingly '1.0' both in interface and ability. Voyager catalogs, for example, are rigid and unforgiving for the searcher uninitiated in the arcana, particulars, and exceptional cases of the particular library's catalog in question; the interface is also unattractive, boring, and much less usable than, say, the advanced search interface for Google Books.

It is this that Casey was reacting to on his blog.

Casey, like so many librarians since the late 1990s, wants a library OPAC, and, indeed, a wide suite of library services (services both online and in 'real life') that *are not* ugly or rigid. Library 2.0 is a movement to establish and promote elegant, very useful, and very usable library tools and services. These will tend to be highly customizable, personalizable, and collaborative. These, like the new tools of Web 2.0, will tend to meet user demand for information management and search tools that are taggable, hackable, geolocative, social, permissive, mashable, and that get the job done not just *better than* it has been done before, but in ways that were not entirely imaginable before the advent of the social Web.

The dawn of the semantic web

Library 2.0 is a precursor to Library 3.0. Using 2.0 to describe things (including libraries) has gone from trendy, to common, to dull. But when we look at the real *weight* of the concept, to see what it can do and how, we find that library use of Web 2.0 tools to engage communities is preparing us for Web 3.0.

Now the meaning of this term, Web 3.0, is not universally agreed upon. In some quarters (Peters, 2007), it is meant to designate a three (or four or more) dimensional information space, which would possibly be experienced in ways similar to that of our time in Second Life (which we will be covering in much greater detail in Chapter 6). Others have used the term as a quick pointer toward a semantic web, which is based on the idea that items on the Internet will be self-descriptive to the point of (at least) *seeming* intelligence, and able to fully integrate and understand the provenance of other resources, whether the information comes in audio, video, text, or *other* (Evans, 2007b). The upshot to this second view of Web 3.0 is that people will be able to ask natural language questions and get consistently good answers back *from machines*. Given that those machines will be running protocols written by humans, this phase in the evolution of the Internet will be a very important and game-changing one. As Tim Berners-Lee says of it (Fischetti and Berners-Lee, 1999):

> I have a dream for the Web [in which computers] become capable of analyzing all the data on the Web – the content, links, and transactions between people and computers. A 'Semantic Web', which should make this possible, has yet to emerge, but when it does, the day-to-day mechanisms of trade, bureaucracy and our daily lives will be handled by machines talking to machines. The 'intelligent agents' people have touted for ages will finally materialize.

If Web 3.0 is successful, we might well imagine it pulling the rug out from under our bookcarts, so to speak. The *coup de grâce* to an old and ailing profession? As one metadata librarian once put it, 'If I'm doing my job right, it will put the reference department out of business.' As an old reference guy myself, I'm not yet ready to let her win, despite Stephen Wolfram's lean mean new semantic machine, the Wolfram Alpha engine. It's just another tool to me.

Much of this book is concerned with Library 2.0 in terms of its effects on our communities and what we can do with Web 2.0 to better reach and serve them; but my prejudice is that the widespread or ubiquitous adoption of Web 2.0 is creating the kind of environment in which Web 3.0 will be nourished by standards of meaning set by social networks and communities of interest. Web 3.0 is a long way from ripe, but the bud is already on the vine. We have to become concerned with the steps we can take to successfully graft libraries onto the tree.

2

New library users

As information technology has changed – just take a look at Figure 2.1 – so has the nature of the needs of our patrons. Patron expectations about what constitutes a library is in the process of great change as well. Many of these changing expectations reflect the nature of their experiences with Web 2.0. Interactivity and mobility are the most obvious and active fronts for this change in our library users, and *sociability*, if you will, is an important aspect of interactivity. The 'new library users' are a subset of all of our library users, but they are a vocal and influential subset. This is not strictly a generational or subcultural difference, because as online tools have evolved into increasing ease and usability, information seekers across all demographics have also come to expect online services to be universally easy for them to use.

One need only look at results from the Pew Internet & American Life Project (2005) to see the range of age spans of the 72 percent of Americans that use the Internet, and of the variety of uses they have for the Web, many of which are Web 2.0 tools like blogging, texting, and interactive media use (Hanson, 2007: 43). According to the Pew report, over 20 percent of people aged 70 and older 'go online' – and the usage for younger generations, those in their 60s and 50s right through to teenagers, floats around 80 percent. As the cheerful image in Figure 2.2 suggests, both old and young are increasingly active online. The numbers are different in

Figure 2.1 We have had time to become accustomed to technology, now

Great Britain, but there is a similarity in a strongly upward trend in general usage. From the turn of the century to 2007, Internet usage across the total population of Britons jumped up about 40 percent (Internet World Stats, 2007).

None of this is to dismiss the problems that still exist in providing access to all. Rosenberg (2004: 633) points to

Figure 2.2   Books, machines, grandpas, and babies

Source: Marc W.F. Muerrens (*http://upload.wikimedia.org/wikipedia/commons/f/ f2/Marc_nils_home_office_2004.jpeg*).

statistics that show 'clear demographic gaps' remaining in Internet access. Access inequalities linger; and by pointing out that most public libraries give patrons access to the Internet, I would not want to understate the problems with access that remain. Clearly, however, if someone in the western (or westernized) world wants access they can in the majority of cases get access – and that is thanks in no small part to the fights fought by our public librarians.

The new library user is a post-Gates Foundation Grant library user. This is a population, in the wealthy West, in which even the poorest citizens have gotten used to the idea of being able to freely and openly walk into a public library, sit down at a computer terminal, and search the World Wide Web for whatever information they might want to find, be it an essay about the chemical reactions that cause Mentos candy to explode when in contact with Diet Coke (is that education?), be it pornography (is that information?), or be it a streaming video of a performance of *Othello* (is that entertainment?). What was once the domain of only the most wealthy has become more common than corn syrup; and even if she cannot read, the new library user can access an enormous amount of audio and visual information (including many free online audio books through projects such as Project Gutenberg, the Internet Archive, and Librivox).

But libraries the world over (not, however, all libraries in the world) have made online services and online access an important part of basic library services in the last fifteen years or so, Gates grants or not, and library users (no matter their age or income) have thereby been transformed into a different kind of patron. Clearly library services vary even within states or regions; the Indian public library system shows a non-uniform state of development from region to region, for instance, which is dependent on local political conditions, funding, and collective will (Dasgupta, 2000).

Our patrons now have different expectations of librarians, and we have different expectations about what we owe to them. A measure of our worth may be the measure of how well we transition into Library 2.0 without complaint; those of us left whining about the changing demands and changing demographics of our changing population of library visitors will find, quite soon enough, that we have a quickly decreasing population of visitors (both online and in 'real life') about which to complain. If you hassle them, they'll go elsewhere.

Bald babies, gray grannies

Who are they, these days, these people who still think well enough of us to turn up and ask for guidance in finding and using information? OCLC surveys grant us a glimpse of some of their attributes. The OCLC's findings on 'Perceptions of Libraries and Information Resources' (2005) show that (the parts referred to below are the different parts of the report in which more detail is laid out):

- Respondents use search engines to begin an information search (84 percent). One percent begin an information search on a library website. (Part 1.2)

- Quality and quantity of information are top determinants of a satisfactory information search. Search engines are rated higher than librarians. (Part 2.6)

- The criterion selected by most information consumers to evaluate electronic resources is that the information is worthwhile. Free is a close second. Speed has less impact. (Parts 3.1 and 3.4)

- Respondents do not trust purchased information more than free information. The verbatim comments suggest a high expectation of free information. (Part 3.4)

- Library users like to self-serve. Most respondents do not seek assistance when using library resources. (Part 2.4)

- Library card holders use information resources more than non-card holders, and they are more favorably disposed to libraries than non-card holders. (Parts 1.1, 1.4 and 3.7)

- Age matters sometimes. Sometimes it doesn't. Responses are sometimes consistent across US age groups, suggesting age-independent preferences and practices. Familiarity with e-mail is an example. In other areas, responses vary considerably by the age of the respondents. For example, young US respondents are much less likely than those over 65 to agree librarians add value to the information search process. (Part 2.6 and all Parts)

- The survey results are generally consistent across the geographic regions surveyed. Responses from the United Kingdom showed the largest range of variations from other regions surveyed. (Part 5 and all Parts)

Our younger patrons, particularly students, have a focus on speed. Surveys show that when patrons are pleased with libraries, they are often pleased with the speed and efficiency of the services we offer; a mean percentage of 63.8 percent of library user respondents in India, Australia, Singapore, Great Britain, and the United States decide on whether to use any given electronic information source based on whether it 'provides fast information' (OCLC, 2005: Part 3.1). When patrons are dissatisfied, or when they prefer to use non-library resources, it is often because library resources are not perceived as being fast or efficient enough to meet the users' needs (OCLC, 2005: Part 2). The new library user is a library user interested in cutting into the meat of the matter, not in chewing the fat. Our work is to show that the steps we take (using a clunky catalog, or running our fingers up and down index pages in multi-volume reference sets) are *all* aimed at the meat. Because all the steps we take *are*, aren't they?

Branding libraries as 'get to the meat' places is not especially easy, particularly in light of so many librarians rightly wanting to preserve context and teach critical thinking skills. The 'no fat' or 'bullet point' learning culture that is perhaps on the rise comes to be distinctly at odds with the values libraries traditionally stand guard for: context, process, and criticism really *are not* just fat. There are plenty of discussions about 'library branding' these days, most of which seem to focus on increasing the quantity of patrons visiting libraries rather than the quality of information skills we share with them. This is due partly to the difficulty (politically and practically) of challenging the entire educational culture of whole nations; in the United States, for example, it would mean coming to bared teeth and balled fists with the evangelists of standardized tests and such malarkey.

What does the brand 'library' mean? Think about this: what does the brand 'architect' mean to you? Now you cannot fairly answer a question about what the brand 'librarian' means – you are likely far too close to the subject to give an adequately objective answer – but other people can, and have. It turns out that, again according to the OCLC's Perceptions survey, some 65 percent of library users brand libraries with 'books' – that number jumps up to about 73 percent in the UK (Part 5). Never mind the hundred years worth of cartoon, audio, and film media spoofing the little-old-lady caricature of librarians. It is clear that for most people libraries are seen as houses for books (and to a much greater extent than they are seen to offer services).

Now, knowing what our users have said about their perceptions of librarians, what sort of brand can we build for our profession? Others have asked (and asked, and asked) too. The question is not posed in order to get librarians to do more navel gazing and image management in order to cast themselves as *cool* for the Bebo crowd. This is meant to get you to think about who you and your organization appeals to, and what changes you may have to make if you want your services to reach new markets.

And yes, ladies and gentlemen, we want to reach new markets – we want to control, to some degree, who is seeking us out and using our services. Marketing services or products to segments of the population is a famously difficult and complex agenda. Douglas Rushkoff lays out the history of marketing as sets of increasingly subtle systems of coercion employed by governments and businesses (and even regular folks) to accomplish goals, sell products, or control minds (1999). We coerce others, pushing or pulling their attention, to get certain effects; the history of marketing is a long and very often obnoxious history of deployment of coercive tactics. Like Rushkoff's book *Coercion*, which uses the structure of its own beginning arguments as an object lesson on the methods of manipulation, libraries can use marketing techniques to bring in new patrons for new services *in order to teach them to think critically* about media, about information skills, about organizations, and about the nature of the tactics that brought them into the library in the first place. In a media-savvy, viral marketing world, the library 'brand' might be that of the organization that facilitates the corrosion of thought control. This is the kind of brand we must work for: *Libraries break chains.*

Our new library patrons need to come to an understanding that libraries are no longer dusty warehouses for physical volumes. We are social spaces for self-directed learning. If that is marketable, and if that appeals to the new user, we must make clear the ways that Library 2.0 can serve them. Communities will rise from the stacks as people gather around 'warm' books to trade ideas. If better buildings make better people, then better collections build better communities. Collections bring individuals out from isolation into communities of interest, forming relationships over a shared activity, or shared book, or both.

Architecture and layout do clearly impact our behavior. From the very finite and practical questions of our ability to move and act within a space (whether you have to squat over or sit on a toilet, and whether that toilet is in its own room or in a common room, for example, has an immediate impact on the way we meet our bodily needs), to the very abstract issues concerning space, lines, color, and inspiration (*I love the way I feel when I look through the windows in the lobby of the planetarium*), architecture has a real affect on the way we live. Collections, too, impact behavior, as does the layout of collections. Fail to develop an interesting collection and interesting people will cease visiting your library.

Bricks to bits

A rather serious problem with most descriptions of Library 2.0 is that we get pointed to particulars, to specific attributes of a so-called 2.0 service, which are used as cases to metaphorically describe the whole. A whole definition of Library 2.0 seems lacking, though many librarians continue to write about it, and to attempt to define it. What is it, we must wonder, in the abstract? To quit our description of examples and to define it clearly, even if that means the employ of some annoying neologism, might be worthy work; but that's not what this book is about. A history of the ideas that have built up to this current stage of library service would be utterly useful for librarians charging out further, out into Web 3.0.

Interactivity on the Web has come to be defined by tagging, commenting, rating, and other tools for sharing opinions or responses. Search engines like Search Wikia even allow users to rank results for relevance or quality in a five-star system (Evans, 2007b). Amazon.com has long allowed its users to use star ratings for books (and music, software, clothes, tools, and other products), and to write reviews, and this has created a space in which online communities have grown up and flourished around books, music, and goods. The new library user is one who is used to being able to contribute, comment, and lend the weight of their personal responses to websites and services. They interact. So: give them interactive spaces, and take the collection out of the two-dimensional flat page and into four-dimensional activities.

Tagging, most famously exemplified by del.icio.us and Technorati.com, lets users add descriptive terms to websites, books, articles, or other pieces of information presented through the Web without relying on controlled vocabularies. Tags show us how the users of a website describe it, and it also allows users to search for information with more natural or intuitive (rather than controlled and specialized) language. Tagging may be seen as a response to the perceived exclusivity of established organizational schemes. Why learn someone else's descriptive terms when you can create your own, on the fly, informally, without permission, and especially when such loose descriptors actually make more sense to information seekers using said resource? No one (except, perhaps, librarians) really wants to consult the Library of Congress subject headings just to find some arcane, parsed, and wildly particular turn of term instituted by category-mad information mavens. People want to use simple and common language to search, even if it leads to results that are too often inexact, inappropriate, or irrelevant. Tags are about searchers owning their own search terms.

The mobility of information has also had a very important impact on the way our patrons seek and use information. With the mobility of websites and web-based applications through widgets (or gadgets, depending on your politics), RSS feeds, and mobile computing devices (from laptops to cell phones), our patrons have come to want instant access to any (not all) of the world's information now and here: immediately, in their pockets, accessed quickly with minimal clicks. Searchers want information to be mobile, like they are.

As the Web has evolved into a more interactive and mobile information environment, so too have information seekers come to expect that information should be delivered to them in any number of formats in a way that allows them to use the information interactively and to use the information in a mobile fashion.

Their use of a book, for instance, should not be tied to using that book in any particular physical place; they may wish to view it on the web, take a physical copy with them, or get passages delivered to their phones. The patrons in Figure 2.3, as an example, seem to be handily able to move between physical and online media. Indeed, some readers may prefer to read whole novels, like Rin's 2007 bestseller *If You*, in the original medium (Onishi, 2008). They also want

Figure 2.3 Patrons working with information in multiple media

Source: Ziko-C (*http://upload.wikimedia.org/wikipedia/commons/7/72/Wpm02_09.JPG*).

to interact with the information, and in the case of books, they may wish to rate or review the book in a library catalog, make notes on a digital copy of the book, or add tags and hyperlinks to other information sources in the book's catalog record. Douglas Rushkoff's 2002 novel, *Exit Strategy*, was an early popular example of so-called 'open source' fiction. The novel existed as a web page that anyone could log into and add text to the document, which would later be edited and added to the mariginalia of the final form of the novel. We will find that library users are increasingly disposed toward *participating* in this kind of thing.

The new library patron wants a library that responds to the new information environment. Libraries will have to let go of some nineteenth- and twentieth-century habits to keep up with these twenty-first century demands. Centralized, controlled vocabularies will have to cede turf to tags. Stacks dear and precious enough to keep closed and locked will need to be digitized wholesale. Physical access to reference services will have to make room for mobile, web-based answer agents. The nasty old habit of defacing books by creating marginalia will become magnified as patrons find new ways (mostly by way of social catalogs, QR Code, and RFID read-write systems) to addend, amend, and notate books and other items.

Hackers are old hat

Twenty-first-century library users may indeed be shifting toward a new social ethos, turning from the old individualistic lone-researcher of the era of the Protestant Ethic that drove capitalism so well for so long, toward a new Hacker Ethic set to fuel the maturation of the Information Age. Pekka Himanen (2001) posits that as the Protestant Ethic fades as a dominant cultural milieu in the West, millenials are coming of age in a developing global culture which is beginning to work on the principles of a Hacker Ethic: principles of play, exploration, social connection, and exuberant enthusiasm may, for the new generations, be overturning centuries of values based on duty, selfless work, and guilt.

If this is truly the case, we must look more closely at who hackers are and what they do. Hacking is widely understood to be a naughty thing to do. It entails sneaking into places you have no permission to be and fiddling around with information that does not belong to you, right? Greasy video game enthusiasts do this late at night, after they get through stealing petrol from their neighbors tanks and worshipping the devil; we all know the story. Hackers have variously been demonized (both in popular media and by government agents) and glorified (again, both in popular media and by government agents – take the Defcon/Black Hat conference in Los Angeles for example, where even a Principal Deputy Assistant Secretary of Defense for Networks and Information Integration may rally the crowd, working to enlist their help against America's enemies) to the point of mythos. But hackers know information, and when hackers are portrayed as heroes, it's usually for their 'information wants to be free' techno-libertarian-populism ethics and (a-*hem*) praxis. Well, information *is* free at the library.

These days, maybe, hacking is not taken quite so seriously by Joe Sixpack – hackers are either losers or the top secret rulers of the world, but either way it has little bearing on my finishing this here tall can of lager. Hacking, as a verb, means to tinker and rework, loosely speaking. Libraries can become outposts of meta-hacking: zones where programs and collections, people and instruction, come together to make it possible to learn how to hack more and hack better. A new slogan to employ: 'Libraries build communities of 'chain-breakers.'

The presumption that a hacker-informed ethos, leading to a mobile, instant, and ubiquitous network serving a mobile, info-skimming, and shallow-reading information seeker, is a good thing for libraries to promote is a heavy presumption indeed. This is all leading to something, though; librarians cannot individually or collectively turn back the tides of culture, but if we embrace the changes we see, maybe we can shape the future a little and ensure that some of our values get carried along inland with the sea.

The new library user, well, maybe she's a little bit weird. But the world is weird, and getting a lot weirder. Preparing for Web 3.0 may mean that in some ways we are preparing to prepare for the techno-social singularity that the transhumanists go on about. Let's not get caught twiddling our thumbs this time around.

> ... As we come to rely on computers to mediate our understanding of the world, it is our own intelligence that flattens into artificial intelligence. (Carr, 2008)

Part 2
The People's Web

3

Folksonomic exchanges: authority of the people

We could say that a tag is *a unit of conceptual indication in a folksonomic system of organizing information*. Folksonomic? A folksonomy is positioned roughly opposite of taxonomy (see Figure 3.1) in the spectrum of authoritatively controlling the terms we use to describe subjects and identities in that it is an informal and 'horizontal' way of organizing ideas and information rather than a structured and hierarchical system. Taxonomies, we could say, 'try to have all the answers,' while folksonomies 'make up the answers as they go along.' Folksonomy is open to the folk: to quote Ellyssa Kroski, 'Metadata is now in the realm of the Everyman' (2007).

Tags give us the potential to arrange information in local, user-centered systems, in a way that stiff-and-universal taxonomies cannot. However, tags are easy to use poorly, partly because they are so *easy to use*. Taxonomies are logical, systematic, processual. Taxonomies, we might say, are a lot harder to use sloppily than tags are, which, indeed, is their great strength. Taxonomies are for long-term and professional use, and the possibility remains open that folksonomies, too, will show their mettle in the long term as professional-grade ontological tools for handling information management tasks. Kroski points out that this 'grassroots organizational scheme' we know as folksonomy is a 'nonhierarchical ontology that is created as a natural result of user-added metadata ... it is an

Figure 3.1   Hierarchy in taxonomies

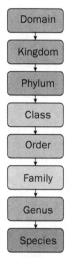

Source: http://upload.wikimedia.org/wikipedia/commons/9/96/Scientific_
classification.png.

organically created taxonomy' which develops over time, according to user need (2007: 94). As long as organizations grow, there will continue to be a need for new users to add new data, and, in that light, tags appear to be nothing short of inevitable. A simple dichotomy between folksonomy and taxonomy that would paint a taxon as a professional or authoritative unit of info-organization while showing tags to be the work of amateurs or crass masses of unskilled hobbyists, therefore, is unfair and inaccurate. Tags are for specialized use; and folksonomies move and evolve more quickly than traditional taxonomies, but one is by necessity no more respectable than another. They have different uses, is all. Tagging can be as logical and processual as taxonomies are, but there may be multiple logical systems for categorizing information and multiple processes for doing so for every individual tagger; it would be unfair to paint tagging too quickly as a haphazard enterprise.

Even in a taxonomic system like Library of Congress subject headings, there are degrees of greater and lesser usability. Wolf points out a choice libraries can make in terms of the OPAC for their ILS, whereby a subject search that brings back no results in the subject headings list can generate a 'no matches' error message or a 'kinder' result of an alphabetical list of subject terms 'that surround the heading entered' (2006: 34). Working with taxonomies is absolutely necessary and should not be abandoned just because tag clouds are more intuitive for some users. We are not in the business of guesswork. But we are in the business of access.

A more detailed exploration of taxonomies we must leave for other writers; now let's look closely at tags and, to begin, their weaknesses. Kroski's summary of the downfalls (both potential and actual) of tags is well worth reading. She writes about the lack of precision, lack of hierarchy (no fine tuning through 'parent–child' categories), lack of recall (that is, a folksonomy cannot return all resources about cats if different cat-items are tagged with differing cat-tags, one with kitty and one with pussy, for example), and other problems (2007: 99).

These recall problems also represent a serious lack of synonym control. Meredith Farkas reminds us that synonym control, or 'pulling together all of the terms referring to a given concept under a single authorized term,' is something that taxonomies do very well (2007: 137). Folksonomies also trip, seemingly irreparably, over polysemes (mole the animal? mole the skin growth? mole, Avogadro's number?), as Farkas notes. Folksonomies cannot even yet gather lexemes together: the tags *jumps, jumped, jumper*, remain effectively unrelated and invisible to each other under current tagging systems. Farkas also points with hope toward some possibilities for fixing the necessary messes that folksonomies make. Collaborative filtering may be one way to do this, because it can tie groups and individuals together according to the tags they use. Search Wikia is an excellent example of a collaborative search engine that aims to give users the ability to tag communally and be linked by sharing terms specific to their own communities of interest (COIs) (Evans, 2007b).

Simple 'user agreement,' an informal contract to use tags in particular ways to increase precision, can also work, especially with smaller or more closely-knit online communities. Hypothetically, members of a UFO investigation group like the Mutual UFO Network (MUFON) may all agree to use the tag *RAF* instead of a variety of tags like *air-force*, *r_air_force*, *roy-af*, or *aforce* to identify items related to the Royal Air Force. This strategy requires open communication and cooperation among the group of users, and more than a little 'radical trust' that individuals will not actively work to spoof the system. This is, of course, an area of vulnerability where users outside the community could consciously sabotage tags and, therefore, search results.

There are many and varied strategies for mitigating the damage or inefficiency caused by the weaknesses of tagging, but there is no panacea for the problem. Unique exactitude in language, one and only one meaning for each term (sememes), does not currently exist in either folksonomic or taxonomic systems. Human language is not computer language, and is not mathematical. Language-based organizational schemes will probably never be precise enough to make automated information management systems completely immune to ambiguity – though efforts toward building a semantic 'Web 3.0' that can get closer to such precision are well under way.

Taking care with tags

For reasons spelled out above, it is very important to think carefully about your tags before you start deploying them without an overarching vision or strategy. Sometimes in the creation of a tagging scheme, a tag makes sense in the short term, or you think that it will once you have your pattern solidly established. But tenuous plans are easily forgotten, and, dare we say it, those at home with the tools of Web 2.0 are often easily sidetracked and massively distractable. You will not remember what you intended to do, and soon you will be dealing with a roiling mess of disparate words sloppily slung toward half-remembered web objects. Again: tags are easy – and that is their danger. Easy to create, easy to deploy, and hard to manage once deployed.

(Tags can be sexy, too. When information visualization techniques are applied to social tagging, tag popularity is ranked with font size, color, dimensionality, or other effects. The example in Figure 3.2 shows world population as weighted tags.)

There are solutions. The split between folksonomy and taxonomy is too often airily and quickly summarized and dismissed in the literature without due and diligent

Figure 3.2   Tag cloud of relative world populations

Source: Warren A. (*http://upload.wikimedia.org/wikipedia/commons/7/78/World_Population.png*).

application of librarians' skills to the use of tags. With that in mind, here is a four-tier strategy for using tags well: Sketch, Test, Pair, and Talk. We'll consider an evolving library program that is working to tie the library in as a resource for local zymurgists.

Sketch

Sketch out the way you want to use tags in your project. This is your time to brainstorm. You will need to think about what it is you need to tag and the nature of the tags you wish to use to describe those items. This sketchy model will only ever be approximate, but it is an important tool to help you think about your strategy. What is your tagging need? Are you tagging items for writing an article, for planning a youth program, or for proposing the construction of a new building? Be specific now: what are you trying to accomplish? If you are working on a program that brings the pub and the library together, you will need tags for different kinds of drinking books (Does Kingsley Amis get his own tag? Fiction vs. Mixology vs. Home Brewing Techniques vs. Commercial Distillation?), different kinds of drinks (resources on ales, lagers, whiskeys, and kir, you know), tags related to personality or personomy (you need a tag to alert the keynote speaker, your red-jowled wine-geek of a mayor, of items related to her topic of choice – the history of rural winemaking in Staffordshire. The tag 'mayor' may do), and logistical tags (for noting places that rent out folding chairs, couriers for the rented glasses, and cleaning services). If you don't have a plan sketched out before you start, the likelihood of ambiguity (read: noise) in your tags will be greatly increased. Just tagging online maps tracing the trade routes for grapes in Western England, for example, as 'wine' would lead to confusion when the 'wine' tag also brings up catalog records, webliographies, and mp3 files that six different people need for a dozen different reasons. Such confusion does not move your program forward, so sketch out a plan while you still can.

Test

Test tags wildly. You need to create preliminary tags for a wide variety of items, and to see how the tags you are developing fit the need. An important part of this test phase is, as will happen when the stakes are larger later, using your tags on random and unexpected items. You may plan to have a partner librarian e-mail items to you based on random 'googlemancy' techniques (like web searching for a term arrived at by selecting the first word on a randomly opened page of a book, then consistently going to a site three clicks deep), or add such random items to a shared del.icio.us account for your later tagging. This method – forcing your tags to cope with unexpected items that will not neatly fit into the scheme you've already sketched out – strains your model for tagging and forces it to become more agile and more flexible. You can see the weak spots now and redesign your tag strategy, rather than being hit hard later when it matters more. True, testing may never strain your model to the degree that 'the real world' will, but it should at least show the most obvious breaking points.

Pair

Use categories with your tags if possible. Categories are a bit like old-fashioned file folders, or the folders for bookmarks (or favorites) you may still have in a web browser. Categories allow you to create an upper-level descriptor for an item that is usually visually more obvious and primary than the numerous tags which may be appended to the same item. For an example, the major blogging platform Wordpress provides categories in addition to tags; in this way you may organize a blog post under the category 'mayor's speech' and with the tag 'grapes.' Items under the category 'mayor's speech' can have *any* tag associated with it, and can also be simultaneously filed under another category, like 'homebrew books.' Clearly, associating an item (or a blog post) with many, most, or all the categories would be to make categorization itself meaningless. If you do not have access to a category or foldering system, consider pairing tags in other ways. You might pair a tag with a number to designate degrees of relevancy or importance. You might co-tag an item with a descriptor and a date. The more you do to provide referential context for your tags, the more you pair them (or triple-tie them) to meaningful anchors of data or language, and the more work your tags will be doing for you. They will be corralled into greater precision whether they like it or not.

Talk

Communicate with your patrons and with other librarians about the nature and scope of the information to be tagged. This strategy can be used by anyone, and when presented to and taken up by your patrons, this fourth tier changes to something like 'communicate with your peers and your librarians about the nature and scope of the information to be tagged.' In our pubs and libraries program example above, we would want to clue in all the major stakeholders, including the mayor, the librarians, the barkeeper, the zymurgists, the brew historians – everyone participating in the program that has a reason to manage information about the development and production of the program. This talking does not have to be strictly democratic, or equitably networked, nor does it need to proceed from consensus; we are not interested here in promoting some general politics or philosophy of communication – we are interested in communicating effectively so that our information is manageable and usable and useful to us. Major players in a project need to, at least, understand the broad-brush strategy for handling information, for use of tags, for foldering into any extant categories. And no amount of 'talk' will prevent free actors from making mistakes in (or even worse, pranking or vandalizing) the tagging system. No amount of clear communication about the type of tags to use will prevent some excitable someone from tagging a news article with the term 'fucking brilliant pint poured by deGroFF @ rainbowroom!!' and that is something librarians will have to get used to swallowing. The ultra-personal tag, useless to the community, is a necessary price of 'keeping found things found,' as Susan Gibbons reminds us (2007: 71). 'The value of social bookmarking systems is diminished when there is an abundance of highly personalized tags,' she writes; but the value only diminishes for the group. For the individual user, such tags may increase the value of the resource described. Balancing the needs of the group and the individual will be difficult, and frankly it is doubtful that your patrons or participating community members will care as much about your (or their?) tagging strategy as you do. After all, you are the librarian, so it is your job to get crazy-eyed geeky and worked-up over the minutiae of folksonomies – not theirs. Those you serve will simply want it to work. So talk with them about it.

The best popular exemplar of tagging on the Web has long been del.icio.us. From the site's 'about' page:

What is del.icio.us?

del.icio.us is a collection of favorites – yours and everyone else's. You can use del.icio.us to:

- **Keep** links to your favorite articles, blogs, music, reviews, recipes, and more, and access them from any computer on the web.

- **Share** favorites with friends, family, coworkers, and the del.icio.us community.

- **Discover** new things. Everything on del.icio.us is someone's favorite – they've already done the work of finding it. So del.icio.us is full of bookmarks about technology, entertainment, useful information, and more. Explore and enjoy.

del.icio.us is a **social bookmarking** website – the primary use of del.icio.us is to store your bookmarks online, which allows you to access the same bookmarks from any computer and add bookmarks from anywhere, too. On del.icio.us, you can use **tags** to organize and remember your bookmarks, which is a much more flexible system than folders.

You can also use del.icio.us to see the interesting links that your friends and other people bookmark, and share links with them in return. You can even browse and search del.icio.us to discover the cool and useful bookmarks that everyone else has saved – which is made easy with tags.

All you need is a browser and an internet connection.

(*http://del.icio.us/about/*, 2008)

Very useful in a world where the amount of information is growing exponentially. When you find something, you can bookmark it so that it is easy to find again later. But how is this more advantageous than the bookmarks stored in your web browser? This is where the 'sharing' or social element of taggable bookmarks begins to become very important. The social nature of what you have saved makes it easier for others to find and use what you have found useful, and this is the meat of the tool for librarianship. Tags are public (in del.icio.us, Library Thing, and most other social bookmarking services), and completely viewable by anyone looking at the sites you have saved. If the tag is unique, it will not take your patron to any other sources tagged with that tag (because the tag, being unique, describes only one resource); most tags are not unique. If a website reviewing this book is tagged with 'folksonomy,' and an information seeker clicks that tag, she will be taken to results for all resources tagged with the term 'folksonomy' (16,178 items in del.icio.us as of this writing). Each saved item gives the number of others who have saved it, and the other tags associated with it. A hint is even held out, as in Figure 3.3, that finer and subtler levels of patterns may emerge as social bookmarks 'organize themselves.'

Like del.icio.us, iubo is a social bookmarking service, but it is newer to the game and brings new tools. Like del.icio.us, iubo allows users to save items and tag them, but it also goes further with the integration of web widgets and search filters

Figure 3.3 del.icio.us pattern emergence?

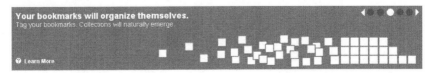

Source: del.icio.us / Yahoo! Inc.

to allow for more precise organization of larger information sets in any online medium. Del.icio.us still stands as an archetypical example of tagging in action, but newer services like iubo will force greater agility and increased innovation in the traditional tagging and bookmarking sites. If they are going to remain relevant and competitive, del.icio.us, Technorati, and the rest will have to keep an eye on the likes of iubo and others seeking to integrate widgets into social bookmarking (Evans, 2009).

Getting back out of the box

It boils down to this, for librarians: sharing pages (and describing them with tags) means that your patrons can see what you have found useful and why you think it is useful for them to use, too.

I once worked at a library where a blue plastic box was shoved halfway back in the middle drawer of the reference desk. It had a neat, typed-up, printed-out, and taped-on paper label: Websites. You crack the box open, cough the dust cloud away, and flip through a mini vertical style file folder system for index cards – each card organized by subject, roughly, then alphabetized by site title. Each card had a URL typed under the title, then a brief description of what was to be found at the typed resources. No mention of how it could be used, what particular projects it was good for, or what other resources (print or otherwise) might work well in tandem with the site – not enough room for all that on an index card, after all.

Some prankster put a Post-It on the box: 'Anybody use this?? I'll bet these sites get lonely in here, un-hyperlinked as they are ...' del.icio.us (and other social bookmarking tools like it), take the links off of the index card and put them into their native territory – the Web. Transferring webliographic information from the Web to print is a laborious, inefficient, and largely useless project – especially when you consider that you will need to put that webliographic data back into the Web in very short order to make any use of the data at all. This book itself, by the way, would be best read online – fully bristling with live hyperlinks, text searchable, and every word indexed – and I hope that the majority of you are reading it in electronic format now. If not, you've got a lot of URLs to type in. So let web resources *be* web resources. Don't hobble them by taking them unnecessarily into a less useful format.

The most important result of this is that your resources are shared. If it's in a box, one person at a time can see it, but if it's on a network, many can. It may seem an obvious point (after all, this is the whole *point* of the Internet), but this aspect of tagging highlights how we can make our bookmarked resources work harder for our communities. So take out that dusty box of links from 2001, look at each index card, and ask: how can I make this information (not this card) work harder? The answer will very probably have something to do with social bookmarking.

Tagging is about informally describing resources (1) so that one can find and use the resources again, and (2) so that others can find them based on tag searches. Development of some logical system for tags is very important, as illustrated in our pub program example above. The seeming casualness of tagging can distract us from the fact that our early tag choices set precedents which will necessarily shape our future descriptions of resources.

Not all social bookmarking systems (tag operating systems, if you will) use the same procedures and protocols. Some require a comma between tags (tags, social networks, arphids), where others use a space to separate tags (tags socialnetworks arphids). These disparate systems, like the nature of folksonomy itself, are not standardized. There are no universal conventions, and there is no such thing as an International Body of Folksonomic Conventions to set the pattern that the world should use in describing tagged information online. We are making up the conventions as we go along. This is both good and bad – good because we still have the freedom to retain local or organizational or personal control over the way we tag, but bad in that confusion can creep into the meanings we assign to our descriptor terms. Take the above example; having to eliminate the space between the terms 'social' and 'networks' creates a new term: 'socialnetworks.' This, prior to its necessity in a space-based tag identity framework, was not a useful term – the idea was represented with 'social networks' or perhaps 'social-networks.' It is the space as the operator (indeed, as a signifier of new or next meaning) that causes the term 'socialnetworks' to come into existence. When tagging a review of some new application that bridges Facebook and Second Life, one is likely to use the usual format: two words (social networks) in the description, and if the space signifies *new tag*, we end up with two tags instead of one – both of which are essentially useless without the other (*second* as a tag, and *life* as a tag).

Tagging on the open Web is one thing, but what about tagging within our library websites, catalogs, and intranets? LibraryThing for Libraries has developed a way to make exactly that happen, and as of this writing 57 public and academic libraries are using the LibraryThing code on their websites so that patrons can rate, tag, and comment on library holdings.

One Tuesday night, I had a student rush up to the reference desk looking for information on cutting crown molding.

'I just got the call,' he said. 'I do this on the side, at night.' He was supporting his time in college with an off-the-bed-of-his-pickup-truck business, doing light carpentry, faux finishing, handyman tasks, and he couldn't afford to let the job go just because he was lacking in his miter saw technique. We started searching the catalog, but could find nothing but general carpentry works. Our subject headings had 'molding' listed, but only in terms of casting ceramics and plastics in molds, industrial injection molds – not in terms of baseboards or crown or ceiling moldings (you know, the strips of decorative wood to contrast the wall from the ceiling). This was a classic example of the expertise of librarians falling short in the face of the needs of the real world. Some of those carpentry books had enough to get him started, and we did have something on general box saw applications, so he left well and happy enough.

But I wasn't happy. I went to the Library of Congress subject authority headings website and found nothing for molding there either – again, just casting molds, not even an entry for 'molding, decorative.'

An hour later, a carpentry instructor that I hardly ever see walks into the library to use our pencil sharpener – a slightly asynchronous synchronicity – and I tell him about the search.

'You might try searching under "mill work,"' he says.

Expert carpenters know the words they need to describe what they do better than expert librarians ever will. *Learn* that.

And a note just to tidy this story up. I e-mailed the science and technology librarians at the Library of Congress to get more information, and check myself that I wasn't using their authorities tools incorrectly ... A kindly librarian wrote me back to suggest I 'combine "moldings" with two other subject headings, "decoration and ornament" and "carpentry" in searching.' This works well in the catalog, but not at all in the subject authority records. I have yet to find an authority record for moldings.

Hey librarians, want to reach out to a new potential community of library patrons? Fix this problem, and tell people who work with their hands that you've got their backs.

It is worth the reminding (and, perhaps, the statement of the all-too-obvious) that tags are as yet only text. Combinations of characters, numbers, symbols, or punctuation marks may be tags – but as of this writing, colors, sounds, gestures may not. That is to say, we cannot describe resources with ▬ yet, or with a unit of sound (though we could do so with words like 'gray,' with hexidecimal color codes, or with mathematical notations describing tone). We cannot yet describe a resource, tag it, with a roll of our heads or a sequence of finger-snaps. It is worth imagining the implications of our abilities to do so, however, particularly in light of the nascent gestural computation at work in the world of ubiquitous computing. You've YouTubed Jeff Han's TED Talk, now, and you've seen multi-touch since get folded into iPhones and the BlackBerry Storm, for instance?

Social networking: making it work

It took a little while, but librarians finally began to notice how much their younger patrons using the public computer terminals liked to browse to sites such as Bebo and Friendster in the early-to-mid 2000s. Plenty of librarians reacted with curled lip, dismissing the sites, and the very activity of 'hanging out' with friends through these personal profiles online, as inappropriate for the library setting. Some libraries responded with a knee-jerk slap-down, and banned access outright, either to the sites in question or for teens generally. Librarians began in-fighting, some crying out for free access to these sites in the face of obvious censorship, and others holding firmly to the idea that 'that kind of thing' ought to be done at home. These fights and the struggle to establish a space for libraries in the social spaces online (and to establish a place for these sites within the world of library services) would be a major generational, attitudinal, and cultural fissure in the library world. We are still working through the implications, and are likely to continue our professional in-fighting for at least a while to come. Negotiations are bound to continue for at least as long as it may take for the social dimension of online tools to truly and deeply infiltrate our daily library wares to the point that we are forced to accept it as completely as we have the ILS or the public Internet terminal or the photocopier. Or the pencil.

Social software is at the heart of Web 2.0. It orients the Web toward a dynamic exchange, not just of information through automation, but of contact with other people. Friendster was arguably the first major social networking site to grab the public imagination on more than one continent, starting out in 2002 and reaching its peak in 2004. Its popularity in fast-growing Asian Internet markets may mean that Friendster is not yet out of the running for the top spot. Yet the very phrase 'top spot' seems, in some ways, an outdated notion for the world of social software; it is not just *one* social networking site we use – we use many.

Social elements are active in many Web 2.0 software tools, but these social networking sites are suites of social tools explicitly meant to link people in a variety of ways based on shared interests, shared location, or shared friends. hi5 is an example of a social networking site that has expressly and intentionally exploited smaller international markets for greater long-term gains, drawing in much more of the much less profitable Internet traffic from the 'developing' world. Many users of such sites have profiles on more than one; different sites for different purposes, and different profiles for different purposes, work to enable a more complex identity management paradigm for our library patrons. Which *you* is pre-eminent on Facebook – your professional self, your club-hopping self, your rugby-playing self? Is there a different 'you' represented on MySpace to the one in a Ning workgroup? Is your *'twee' John Peel fan self* dominant, or is your *home-brewed moonshine-swilling Steve Earle listening self* dominant on your Pandora shared-profile? Different profiles for each, perhaps? And, quite likely, different networks for each too.

Just as 'identity management' can be complicated, the story of social networking sites is also complex, intertwining, relatively new, and very relevant. (Meredith Farkas' *Social Software in Libraries* (2007) acts as a great primer for wider issues in the history of library reactions to social software, and she also spends a considerable amount of detail on the particulars of their implementation.)

Preening your feathers and picking your ticks

Libraries would be very hard-pressed to *well* maintain profiles in multiple social networking sites – a presence in one or two is plenty enough to manage. Spreading your efforts too thinly will lead to presences of poor quality and poor service and outreach in multiple sites rather than good service and good outreach in a few or in just one. You will want to choose quality over quantity in these efforts. Just because you may notice your patrons logging into Ning, Friendster (see Figure 4.1 for the friendly Friendster start page), hi5, MySpace, Yahoo! 360°, CyWorld, and Bebo doesn't mean you have to meet all of them in all of those spaces all of the time. Indeed, if you tried to, you would hardly have any time left over to meet them in person at the reference desk, or walk them into the stacks to teach them how the call numbers are ordered.

Figure 4.1   Friendster start page

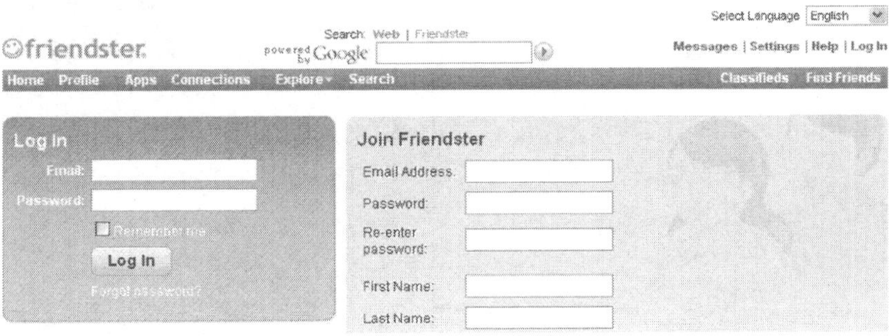

Source: Friendster, Inc.

So which service should you work in? This takes some careful planning and observation. It will require thinking about what your library mission is, what you aim to do and who you aim to reach, and what you currently do and who you currently serve, no matter what your plans for the future may be. Who do you serve today, and how is that group changing? Depending on the kinds of services and outreach you plan to promote through social software, you will find various services supporting certain aspects more readily. For example, Ning works well for active working groups where everyone on the team is sharing information to solve particular problems, which would put it on the shortlist for academic, corporate, or military libraries, for instance. MySpace and Facebook are by far the most commonly used social networking services in the world (these things change, so check Alexa for yourself), and many of their characteristics and formats are widely used by other services. Friendster, MySpace, and Facebook are all similar to each other in function, in many ways, and also share history and users. There is much overlap between the three in the story of their beginnings also, and there will likely continue to be much overlap between users of the three networks into the foreseeable future.

Facebook began as a way for college students to connect with each other and find friends through campus-bound networks (specific to Harvard University, at first). Because of its ability to link people in an informal way, Facebook quickly grew into the premier social networking site for all kinds of organizations in a way that MySpace never has. However, Facebook was only able to become such a broadly popular 'social utility' after it opened membership up to virtually anyone in 2006. It has been able to overcome its earlier marketing as a student-only site to great effect.

Although there were many important innovations made well before MySpace or Facebook appeared, since these two continue to be the pre-eminent social networking sites on the World Wide Web, we will take a close look at how to use these for library outreach and services, but the strategic and tactical points may be abstracted to other social networking sites too. Indeed, with 'social networking' features becoming integrated more often into many other websites and online tools, treating a special profile located on a particular website may soon be a rather old-fashioned way to reach out to your patrons. Nevertheless, since the tactics are abstractable, we can use profile-based social sites as good object-lessons for other types of 'social Web' endeavors.

Before getting into the guts of the process, though, we will take a moment to catch our breath and think about the murky lake we are about to dive into, and say something about new responsibilities.

Social networking, suddenly serious

Imagine this librarian's first experience with MySpace was at a military base library near a dusty, cowpoke town full of manure and tumbleweeds. It was a multi-function library, providing information services to academic communities, families and children, military men and women seeking recreational materials, and information to support the core mission of (as one Squadron Commander put it) breaking things and killing people. It was a busy place, and the staff of the library had a lot to do and many roles to play.

The enlisted men and women and the officers used the library computer labs for a variety of purposes, mostly for fun; and teenagers did too – coming in from the base housing units for the water fountain or soda machine and to spend an hour or two browsing the graphic novels and manga collection, or surfing the Web. MySpace was growing in popularity in 2004, but most parents did not know what it was, what it was used for, or that their children spent so much time on it.

One day, one of the regular patrons, a teenage girl, stopped coming into the library. Very soon, her parents came in to tell the library staff that she had run away – they wanted to find out if there was a way to see what she had been doing online in the library. They had a few clues, perhaps their daughter's MySpace username from some printed and forgotten scrap of e-mail in her closet, and they wanted to see if the librarians could help them find her. There was not much that the librarians could do. They kept no browser histories and they, rightly, had a computer administration system that protected patron privacy. But they did their best to help the parents, searching the Web until the likely address she had ran to (somewhere near San Francisco, California) was found.

The story was no tragedy – a bit of teenage rebellion and angst, soothed by the balm of promised friendships online that, thankfully, turned out to be harmless (if not legitimate) in her case. The parents got in touch with the girl's 'friend' and got her home very quickly.

Incidents like this have brought the world of the Internet and the cultivation of online information skills and the world of libraries (traditionally the places people go to in order to access information) together into a slightly uncomfortable and very personal social network. Libraries are becoming central loci of psycho-cyber-melodramas. Suddenly many new questions must arise:

- Are libraries culpable for the bad things that happen when people 'meet' online if the meeting happens while one of the people is at the library?

- Will libraries be responsible for the safety of their patrons online in the same way they may be responsible for their physical safety in the library's bricks-and-mortar instantiations?

- If libraries are responsible, how do we get to be the good and vigilant guardians that our communities will demand we become?

- Or is it the place of the patrons' legal guardians and caretakers to teach online safety skills?

- If librarians are asked to help clean up the mess of *bad meetings*, as in the above example, where should we draw the line between patron privacy and patron safety?

There will be many more such questions, and many questions with much more complex and subtle answers for librarians to ponder in the near future. But part of building Library 2.0 is becoming familiar with, even if not comfortable with, these issues. The more work we do in this arena now, and the more problems we can solve early, the less damage will be done through ignorance and through the dereliction of duties, including duties both known and unknown. It may happen that an important component of being a 2.0 librarian is managing the library's mediated (and face-to-face) social network with *and between* its library patrons. But I hope not.

danah boyd relates her experience with a fan page she created to celebrate the music of Ani DiFranco, and how it unexpectedly led her deep into the emotional lives of strangers. It is worth quoting at length:

> I still blame myself for the suicide of a young girl. It was a few years ago now. My Ani DiFranco page was everyone's resource and every day, i got letters from young girls who wanted to tell me about how they had been raped by their uncles, who wanted to tell me how they cut themselves every day. Dear god, i cannot tell

you how hard that was. I wrote back, i tried to help. I was often behind in my email and i was a bad correspondent; they always wrote back in minutes. Then there was this girl. She detailed how her mother beat her. She told me about her life. She wrote me every day – i wasn't as good at responding. And then she started talking about suicide. I encouraged her to seek help, i asked her where she lived, i gave her national hotline numbers, i tried to find someone at Hotmail who could help (but we all know how customer service is). She came up with excuses as to why she couldn't. Her letters got more and more desperate. And then they stopped. I kept pinging her. Nothing.

The guilt was ravishing. I didn't even know this girl but i felt so terrible. I made contacting me on the Ani page much harder. I vowed not to start engaging again. I just couldn't handle being involved only when strangers were desperate. It was too much.

Being faced with information overload can be a curse. You want to react, you want to notice. But it can make you exhausted. Worse, it can devastate you. Facebook is giving me the 'gift' of infinite gossip. But i don't want it. I cannot handle it. And i'm not sure anyone's really ready to receive the One Ring. But it sure sounds precious upfront.

Facebook says that the News Feed is here to say. This makes me sad. I understand why they want to provide it, i understand what users are tempted by it. But i also think that it is unhealthy, socially disruptive, and far worse for the users than the lurking employers ready to strike down upon thee with great vengeance for the mere presence of a red plastic cup.

I also think that it will be gamed. Given a new channel for identity performance, people will begin engaging in a new form of impression management. They already write wall posts to be seen – it will be taken to a new level. Their public displays of connection will take on new strength as they seek to make a performance out of the friending act. They will remove friendship statuses in the most dramatic fashion possible, announcing as far as possible about the evilness of the other person. Facebook News Feeds could make [LiveJournal] drama look like child's play. (boyd, 2006)

We must plunge in. We cannot *half serve* our patrons, and serving the patrons of today means serving them, increasingly, within the dimensions of social networks. It pays, therefore, to realize here and now, before we cross the Rubicon, that there will be pain and problems ahead unlike the struggles we have so far been used to; even for a salty inner-city librarian who has to wipe up after knifings in the stairwells, there is an element of this mediated and anonymous pain that is not reconcilable in the usual ways, because it is not even possible to see the results of the conflicts, much less the results of the healing or resolution that may come after the conflict is over. Participation in these new media may force a new kind of emotional distance, an alienation between libraries and their patrons, and a mechanization in our service; let us hope that such things do not have to become professional survival strategies.

Library 2.0 is not for the weak-kneed.

Good practice: how to

MySpace allows for two basic paradigms for representation and communication. There is 'Who You Are' and there is 'Who You Know.'

Who You Are is represented and communicated to others by way of layout choices and content (whether text comments or embedded videos) on your profile page. Colors, designs, spacing, uploaded pictures, font choice, and so on, all go to establish who you appear to be to those viewing your profile. The music playlist establishes a mood for your profile page that suggests something about your identity or interests.

Who You Know is also a choice in the representation of your self – who you choose to friend reflects on who you seem to be, after all. But there are many more issues intersecting 'who you know', because who you appear to be is extremely dependent on which social networks you are couched in, and which roles you play within any of those networks. Who you know may affect who you appear to be according to whether you are seen as a frequent or infrequent commenter, a constant or an occasional blogger, or whether you post pics of last night's debauchery with your mates or never post any pictures from your real life with friends.

MySpace has several characteristics that sustain outreach to friends. First, you can add friends or be added by friends very easily (you also have the option to deny the addition and thereby avoid spam from dubious profiles), and this allows you to connect with a great number of individuals or institutions (the term 'friend' is a technical one in the 2.0 world). Once connected as friends, you can send out bulletins to everyone connected (or 'friended') to your profile. Musicians, writers, and politicians often use this feature to reach everyone in their network at once to push a new book, album, or to get out the vote or spread a tilted message re some divisive issue or other. You can look to the success of Barack Obama's presidential campaign for validation of this latter use of social networks (though he was working in multiple social networking sites, including his own homebrewed my.barackobama.com network).

Comment on a friend's profile by using the 'add comment' link, which is most often found just under their list of friends, on the lower right. Adding comments lets you send a message that can be personal, but comments are readable by anyone who visits the profile, so the personal nature of the connection is always in tension with its very public display. Librarians, libraries, authors, publishers, and bookshops often use this for publicly glad-handing each other, which serves as an immediately visible and automatic plug of services or goods (though this is perhaps lacking in any hoped-for street-cred).

MySpace also has a built-in blogging feature – every profile comes with an attached blog space. This makes it easy for connected friends to subscribe to each other's news posts, and it provides an additional venue for commenting on a friend's profile or the content of her blog. Private messages, much like internal e-mail, are also available, and there is an instant messaging feature. Private messages are (again, like e-mail) an atemporal means of communication, whereas the instant messaging is, of course, instant. Instant messaging is live and text-based – like a phone call with typing instead of talking – and many librarians will be very used to and comfortable with messaging from other services like AOL's messenger service (AIM), Gmail chat, or Meebo.

There is no lack of ways to communicate with others holding MySpace accounts. Where libraries have fallen short is in either ignoring these vectors, or in using them poorly. That is, if you want to use MySpace to reach out to your patrons, you can – the site itself is easy enough for pre-teens to figure out and use. What really seems to be lacking among librarians is a will to make it perform in ways beneficial for library patrons. It is not enough for a library to have a MySpace account, or to build a MySpace profile; it is not enough 'just to be *on*' MySpace. Libraries have to *use* it, and use it well to reach their patrons (not just their *young* patrons, incidentally) and take library services into their patrons' quiet corners of the Internet. Take your library into their spaces (Evans, 2007a).

Thinking about 'who' your library is and 'who' your library knows is very important. Questions to consider:

- Will you friend only recognized library patrons? (How will you verify their status as patrons?)
- Will you friend anyone who asks you to?
- Will you delete friends that spam you? (How will you define spam?)
- Will you never delete any friends, in the hope that a very large number of friends improves your perceived standing in the network?
- Will you post pictures of library events? (Will you seek permissions from pictured patrons?)
- Will you blog about library events, about book reviews, about movies? (What is the scope?)
- How will you use MySpace for reference services or other information requests?
- How will you decide on the aesthetics of your page, including music?
- How will you promote this MySpace blog, and will it be your library's primary blog?
- How will you promote this MySpace page generally to your users?
- How will you determine the effects of this MySpace page on the library (circulation, new visitors, reference requests, etc.)?

There is much to do in a modern library, and keeping a MySpace presence in good order takes valuable time and attention. Planning the amount of time to pay to online social efforts can even affect scheduling. If, for example, your library intends to use the 'send message' feature to take questions about the library or for reference service requests, someone on staff must be prepared to check the MySpace account during set and scheduled periods of time. If your library intends to use the 'instant messaging/call' feature, then someone must remain logged in to the page for some designated period of time every day in case a patron logs in to seek help through this application, and the call feature must dial a working, manned telephone. Failure to follow through on details such as these will lead to patrons regarding the MySpace presence as a token effort to reach out. It will undermine the library's web presence (and the library brand, generally), making it seem less relevant, less potent, and less legitimate. If you want to be there, really be there, and be there in force. And that means that burnout can bite your staff.

Without substantive service and content, your patrons will sicken of the MySpace version of Web 2.0: a glam, gluey, treacle-on-biscuits take on 'friendship' and social networks. It can all start to look too pink, too cute, too Shinjuku-slick to really matter for the daily efforts of librarians or their patrons. There was a time when the library rags, at least in the United States, were all wringing their hands about whether libraries should begin using social networking sites, all the while looking past the more important questions: what can we do with these new tools to better reach our users, and how? And it sounded a lot like libraries were, once again, missing an opportunity to shape the debate. It seemed that libraries of all types were missing their big chances to contribute to the shape of these new social information tools.

But the libraries that were beginning to reach out through MySpace, seemed to be doing so, overwhelmingly, in unimaginative ways. There was a paradigm at work arguing that a glittery page layout would make the library seem cool in the eyes of its millennial patrons, and, after some time, librarians have begun to clue-in to the notion that there can be more to MySpace than glitzy shells of top 40 mp3s and leaving comments on celebrity profiles.

For libraries to put these tools to good use, innovative librarians have to get out of the habit of echo-chambering with other library innovators – they have to demonstrate, in real and concrete terms, how social software can help library outreach. This means that so-called 2.0 or NextGen librarians need to learn the art of mature debate with their supposed antagonists who oppose MySpace and the like – the lack of mature inter-generational exchange runs the danger of creating an incestuous (and perhaps mutant) strain of unrealistic Web 2.0 militancy. These conversations need to be grounded in the reality of good service at the reference desk.

Library profiles in MySpace ought to be used as gateways for community members (or any visitor, from anywhere in the world) to access the library's homepage with all its ready tools. Public libraries can highlight blogs that evaluate anime titles, or that review graphic novels. Link to your webliographies, your catalog, your database tutorials, your subject-specialist profiles. Highlight program news and connect potential participants to the events beforehand. Use the event invitation tools, for example, to invite your 'friends' to book talks, gaming sessions, bitch-n-stitch groups, anime club movie marathons, or any other programs that your patrons might plan in your physical information commons. If your team has the skills, branch out from English and do this in the language communities of your non-native English speaking patrons (see Figure 4.2 for hi5's Turkish pages).

Figure 4.2   hi5 speaks Turkish

Source: hi5 Networks.

It is also very important for your library to *leverage* its social network. Do not try to treat your MySpace profile like it's some sort of island. There are no islands in the Net. Other profiles can be excellent for gathering information resources that your own profile (or library holdings) may be weak in, and linking to them will be crucial for building a relevant network of services for online patrons. Move the best sources of information (whether these are people, organizations, or elected officials) to the top of your friends list. Exploit the reference potential of these networks; if instant messaging chat features are available, then log in during library hours and be ready to take questions through your profile. If you intend to bother at all with social network sites, make sure that you make them work hard for your institution; otherwise, it turns out to be mere play that bears little real fruit for your institution.

If the library profile you work so hard to develop is only used for connecting with other libraries and librarians, then it boils down to hardly more than a professional networking tool, and not even a very good one – go to LinkedIn for your professional back-patting and glad-handing. If your profile is self-congratulatory and, well, tries *too hard* to be cool, it's more likely to fall flat; after all, in 2009 the use of blogs and social profiles is no longer a cutting-edge activity. If you microblog with Twitter or vlog to your community with YouTube, you are not doing anything *special* anymore. Your community may have even come to expect such 2.0 outreach. The real innovation comes in the clever use of these new abilities to serve your patrons, and in how you put the tool to work. Innovation, as always, takes imagination; the 2.0 Web is not pre-packed innovation-in-a-box. Use the tools to exceed the expectations of those you serve.

Library 2.0 is a state of mind, a state of service, an attitude and disposition you carry with you into your service and outreach.

Two samples: libraries doing it right

A great example of an American library using MySpace is the Fort Worth, Texas, public library. It has separate profiles for its various branch libraries, it posts educational resources and games on its site, it links to new music and video recently added to the library collection, and it gives all kinds of real-world contact information for getting help from the library. Patrons (mostly youth) leave comments for library staff, and so do other library systems, and visiting authors. In fact, authors will verge on spam in the amount of comments they leave for librarians. The Fort Worth pages also link to social service oriented and non-profit organizations for issues related to dating abuse, body image, self-esteem, and other topics of special importance to teenagers.

The British Library also has a MySpace presence (at *http://www.myspace.com/britishlibrary*), and even though the library's mission is different to that of the Fort Worth Public Library, its use of MySpace is similar, though not as extensive. It tells a bit about itself – 'The British Library is the national library of the United Kingdom and one of the world's greatest libraries. As well as holding over 13 million books, 57 million patents, 3 million sound recordings, and nearly 1 million newspaper and journal titles, we also have incredible exhibitions, events and late night views' – and also posts a schedule of upcoming events and hosts slideshows and video widgets from recent exhibitions. There is no immediately apparent real-world contact information; indeed, the profile in MySpace seems to be more of an online social (they do maintain friends and friends' comments) advertisement than a true utilization of the social dimension of the Web to press library service. But in any case, it is a very decent profile that does work to market events.

Social networks have many purposes, and some social networks (like LinkedIn and Ning) are specifically geared to work groups, research, and accomplishing tasks. MySpace is not that kind of social network. MySpace is for swapping animated gifs of girls running down the beach, guys dancing in da' club, and commenting on your friends' layouts and general blingyness. MySpace was not designed with libraries in mind.

Facebook, however, as a 'social utility' that spans the *merely* social aspects of networking into projects, political movements, and professional network, is apt to become a very ready enabler of library promotion. LinkedIn is explicitly for professional networking. These are the places you want to profile your library. Is there an information literacy council forming a committee at your trade school? Suggest Ning (see Figure 4.3) as a workspace and represent your reference desk there.

Figure 4.3 Ning, for advanced social networking options

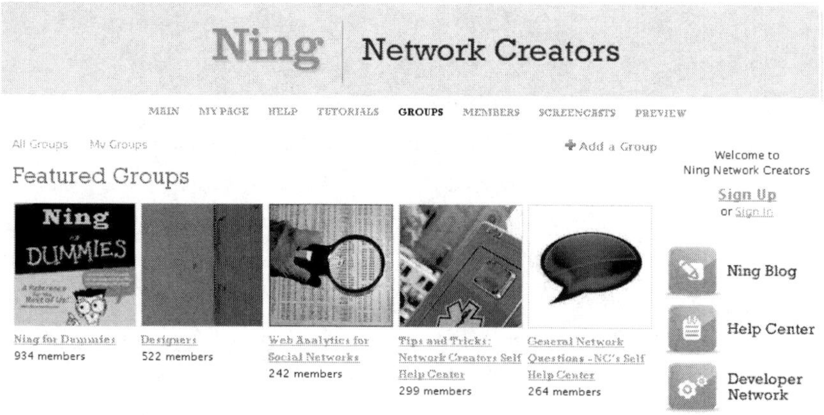

Source: Ning, Inc.

Detailing Facebook

Facebook is similar to MySpace in many ways, but it tends toward a more conservative aesthetic and a much more liberal approach to third-party applications. It differs in several substantial ways.

Users have less control over the look and feel of their profiles. Colors, fonts, and layouts are standard and set, and the only way to personalize your Facebook page is to change the order and number of applications and items posted to your Wall (the Wall is a rough analog to the MySpace comments area). Everything is white and blue. Fonts are not negotiable. Profile pictures are always in the upper left of the page, and user status (online or off) is always directly below the picture. Application boxes in the left column cannot be moved into the right, and items below the 'information' (personal information area) and 'mini-feed' (status updates, changes in news and applications, notices of changes in friends' profiles), cannot be moved into the upper-right of the profile page. Personal status, basic personal information (political and religious views, if you've added them, networks you belong to) are always situated above the mini-feed. It is worth noting that MySpace has unchangeable page elements as well; in Facebook the static nature of the basic template is underscored by the inability to alter it in any way except dragging and dropping allowed fields. (An important note: Facebook shifted into a new layout scheme in late 2008, and though the placement of some items described above relative to others changed, through summer 2009 Facebook has kept its policy of tightly controlling the changeability of basic profile elements.)

Facebook is supple, and infectious in its appeal to third parties in building in-Facebook applications.

Your library, its network

In this age when we must take for granted that the state and corporations are (sometimes legally) watching and listening to us, the social network can place us in political heat.

When the Egyptian police blindfolded, stripped, and beat Ahmed Maher for twelve hours, they weren't just looking to punish *him* for suggesting a nationwide general strike. His proposed act of civil disobedience did bring down harsh punishment on him personally, individually – but the police really wanted access to his Facebook account. The police 'demanded to know the password to his Facebook account and asked for information about the 60,000 people in the group, then threatened to rape him if he would not comply' (Stack, 2008). Those 60,000 people were all joined up with Maher through a Facebook group to help organize and execute a social protest that would have sent a serious message to the Egyptian government. What do you think might have happened to a branch librarian on the outskirts of Cairo had he friended his library's Facebook profile to that of Maher, or to a friend of a friend of Maher's? Do you think librarians are immune to 'little visits' from the authorities? And those authorities, in such a case, may well ask for justifications of controversial or politically sensitive library holdings.

It is well documented in the popular press that in the United States, from 2002 until 2006, security and intelligence agencies (the Federal Bureau of Investigation, and others) could legally visit libraries and demand patron records from librarians. It was illegal, under the new regime, for library staff to inform their patrons that records had been given over, or even to inform patrons that agents may have visited the library. Agents were free to demand circulation histories and web browsing patterns; librarians had no legal way to protest on behalf of their constituents. In 2006 this was overturned with revisions to the original Patriot Act, but this four-year period of teeth-baring between the feds and librarians must not be quickly forgotten.

Librarians at the time did find clever ways to resist, and this was mainly done either by not keeping records that would reveal the information habits of their patrons, or by destroying those records on a regular basis. If the FBI then demanded to know what a patron had been reading, the librarian could truthfully say *sorry, no records exist*. This is still a very widespread tactic; librarians won't soon forget what they had to do to protect the basic tenets of privacy and the freedom to read in their communities.

But Web 2.0 has since burgeoned, and now those who might want to know who we know can use the online networks we participate in to find patterns of association. In the case of our Egyptian progressive, Mr Maher, association with him through the Facebook group he created meant automatic guilt as far as the police had to be concerned.

We cannot know all of the activities, interests, or nodes on the network for the profiles we friend online. Content and purpose of those activities aside (that is, whether we may agree with a particular movement or not), are we responsible for the actions of those we are connected to? Are we responsible for knowing that one of our patrons uses a blog to make hate speech and incite violence? Are we responsible to the other patrons in our network, connected through the library's profile, to vet each and all so that no one gets unfairly connected to another's activities and associates? Of course not. And, on the flip side, do we have a responsibility to shore up support for patrons in our network that try to stand up (for human rights, free access to information, or an end to poverty) and get taken down by the state or by corporations? As major nodes in the social network, ought libraries lend their singular strengths to the causes of free speech and freedom of information online? If we do, some of us may, too, get taken in the night. The bigger the node, the bigger the stakes.

First of all, we cannot know all the aspects and dimensions of all the networks we link to. Secondly, even if we could know everything about the networks we are a part of, we could not possibly preen and peck out all of the lice and grit from the network – networks are holistic, and connections between nodes simply exist. You cannot choose your friend's friends. You can only choose your own. Do you know them well enough, these 'friends' of yours?

Some policy work may be enough to head off major crackdowns here. A statement concerning the library's lack of liability for the actions or comments of those within its network of friends may be enough to halt the stormtroopers in countries under all but the harshest sorts of regimes, but we can make no guarantees there, of course.

Facebook is much more personal than MySpace, in the sense that it directly connects you to other friends, their networks, and their activities; 'your' activities are very much on display in a way that is not designed into the MySpace architecture. Two things arise here. First, it is more difficult to establish your account as an institutional profile because the activities (poking, application addition and activity data, etc.) are oriented toward a personal or individual level. That is to say, MySpace allows breathing room for a certain amount of identity play and anonymity which institutions and organizations like libraries may exploit, but Facebook allows much less of that kind of play in the dimension of identity space. Secondly, deciding who to friend in Facebook, and how to continue friending them (in terms of maintaining the connection or relationship over a longer period of time), becomes more complex in Facebook because it is such an active meta-community. In MySpace, your library can maintain a profile, respond to comments and requests for friends, actively blog, and monitor the instant messaging feature and be fairly well set; in Facebook, however, your library has to evaluate constantly which invitations to shared applications to accept, how active to be on your patrons' wall space, and how to weigh the patron interest that may be lost from not participating in shared social activities, like gaming applications, surveys and quizzes, or joining groups. In short, Facebook demands more attention than MySpace, and will require your library to constantly tend the profile and evaluate new applications.

How to set it up

At Facebook.com you will see a gray box on the right-hand side of the page. The box says 'Sign up for Facebook. It's free and anyone can join.' There are boxes for personal information: name, e-mail address, birth date, sex, and password. So in a few steps, you can sign up as an individual, and use the account either personally or professionally. You can be Sue X, or you can be Sue X The Librarian.

Just under the birth date menu, a small link says 'Why do I need to provide this?' Clicking that, a small pop-up box informs you that your real birth date is necessary 'as both a safety precaution and as a means of preserving the integrity of the site. You will be able to hide this information from your profile if you wish.'

Just beneath that verbiage is another note: 'You are about to create a personal account. If you are here to represent your band, business, or product you should first create a Facebook Page.' The last few words hyperlink to an area where you can create a new organizational Facebook Page. You must select one of three radio-buttoned options: Local; Brand or Product; or Artist, Band, or Public Figure. Selecting Local, a drop down menu has an option for 'Library/Public Building'. Once you select that option, and enter the name of your library, click the blue 'Create Page' button on the bottom. Now you are prompted for all the usual sign-up questions and terms-of-service agreements, unless you already have an account. Once you either create a new account, or log-in with an existing one, the page is officially created for your organization.

You can then begin to tinker.

This 'page' use (rather than 'profile' use) in Facebook gives you some interesting options, including management of your fans, events upcoming, and a discussion board. You can create notes and wall posts with links to helpful resources like subject guides, pathfinders, webliographies, and other kinds of online documents.

A way to promote your library's new Facebook presence for free is to simply set the start or home pages for the web browsers on all of your library's public computer stations to your new page. You may soon begin to see fans popping up.

How to use it at the reference desk

Even in a profile (rather than page), the Wall allows for much reference desk utility. Being able to see questions and comments posted to your profile and to your patron friends' profiles in near real-time makes it easy to respond quickly and publicly. The 'posted items' section is a good place to add commonly referenced online resources; this area can act as a 'ready reference desk' or 'quick reference file' within your profile. When patrons view a posted item, they may click on the 'share' box to the right of the item and send it to their own profile. When they do this, the item *and its share box* go to their profile where it may be seen by their own friends. Posted items (helpful reference links) thereby become social, with the potential to spread in 'viral' fashion from one profile to another.

There will be a temptation to constantly ping back your patrons when you note changes in their status or additions to their walls. There are two main dangers here: one, you will not be able to keep up with hundreds or thousands of patrons changing their profiles constantly, and your attempt to do so may seem cloying, desperate, and insincere; two, even if you have only a few dozen patrons to keep up with, and even if they don't make many changes to their profiles, an inordinate amount of attention from their librarians (especially if such attention strikes a tone that sounds for opportunities to provide services or begs for participation in library programs) will be overbearing and may lead to patrons ignoring messages from your profile or page, or deleting you as a friend, or deleting their status as a fan. Indeed, in this second case, the effect may be magnified if you only have a small number of fans – over-tending your new little garden can kill it before it fruits. Problems following from that include either the tendency to interact with only a small number of your patrons, or interacting with none of them at all.

If you interact with a small number of patrons, you must decide whether this will be a random sampling, catch-as-catch-can approach to interaction, or if this will be a small dedicated group to interact with for specific reasons. If the sampling is random, regular patrons that you really are closer too may feel slighted or snubbed when you don't poke them back. On the other hand, if you regularly interact with a small group, but not other patrons in the network, the library staff may come to seem cliquish and elite.

The other option is simply to swear off ping backs, pokes, and wall comments altogether. But if you are not using your profile or page to reach out and interact with your patrons online, there is hardly any purpose to having a profile in a social network in the first place. The message of 'we're too busy to respond to thousands of tiny changes in who does what on Facebook, so we'll just not respond to your greetings, comments and questions, or pokes *at all*, thanks very much' goes beyond snobbery into, clearly, a dangerous area in which virtual reference service is threatened as sincere requests for help go unread and get heaped onto the 'just more social dross to slog through' pile. At the end of the day, you may have to accept that interaction with the few is better than interaction with the none.

On the other hand, your library staff may be fully capable of investing the necessary amount of time it takes to poke and link and comment with hundreds of library fans. Careful attention to the cost and the benefit is called for here, and noting the relationship between promoting services on a Facebook page and seeing increased database log-ins or book checkouts can be a very gratifying reminder that good service online can build real-world loyalty in direct and lasting ways.

5

Mobile life and QR Code

Lots of rich folks in Europe and North America use mobile devices, from phones to laptops, to stay connected to each other online – that's old news. The newer news is that now the world's poor in the South and the East are picking up phones and accessing the Web, paying for services, and texting each other to get the daily tasks of life done more efficiently, and make a coin or two in the process.

Over 500 million people in China use cell phones (IT Facts, 2007), and the combined estimate of world cell phone use floats somewhere upwards of 90 percent of our 6.6 billion inhabitants (Textually, 2006). Silberglitt et al. (2006) say 'in some developing economies today, wireless communication systems are growing so rapidly that they are in fact replacing landlines as the preferred means of connectivity,' and this is certainly the case in China. The building and maintenance of landlines costs much more than the creation and maintenance of wireless network cells. Partly due to their low cost, and thanks to innovations in microlending, cell phones have become tiny plastic banks where villagers can trade calling card minutes (more liquid than cash itself, sometimes) for favors, labor, or goods.

Many libraries still have 'no phones' policies, banning the use of cell phones outright (see Figure 5.1 for a sample of this silliness). This is unfortunate for a number of reasons. First of all, it is dishonest. There *are* phones. No mobiles

Figure 5.1 No phones!

Source: http://upload.wikimedia.org/wikipedia/commons/a/a6/No_cellphone.svg.

allowed? Well it's in my vest pocket. Try and take it from me, hoss. Secondly, it is future-denial (or worse: present-denial (or worse still: past-denial)) on the part of an organization which lives at the very nexus of culture meeting technology meeting information management: the local library. We should not deny the facts. Our patrons have been using mobiles for some time to communicate, access the Web, and organize personal information; all indicators suggest that the number of mobile users will increase to near 100 percent saturation rates.

But it is most unfortunate that libraries continue to deny phones, because people *use* their phones in so many versatile ways now, and for a lot more than *talking*. Elsewhere (Evans, 2006) I have written about phones as everyware (and that is 'everyware' as Adam Greenfield means it), about the utility of mobiles as mobile computers in library life. Mobile computing leads in short order to ubiquitous computing. Mobile life leads to 'ubicomp.' Attempting to ban phones from our libraries is like trying to ban printed books from the scriptorium in the year 1509; it is a project based on future-denial and present-denial. Our patrons are reading, writing – well, texting, but again, whole novels are composed on *keitai* in Nippon (Hani, 2007) – and searching for information with their phones. While librarians were busy building solid ban policies, the cell phones have spread and mutated into hybrid devices that are closer now to laptops than they are to phones. We would not prevent our patrons from using laptops within our walls, would we? Sadly, some of us might.

This leaves librarians split, and perhaps rightly. How can we fulfill our mission to provide quiet learning spaces if glitzy mobiles bling and blip all day? Many have wondered (and will continue to wonder) whether an attempted ban is the only way to protect the sanctity of quiet study for the studious. The answers, of course, depend entirely on the circumstances of our own communities, buildings, and missions. Libraries have traditionally been sites of quiet study, and a total break with that tradition now, thanks only to the muscle of a majority adoption of an annoying technology, may indeed be a weak response; bowing to phones because we feel we have to would be a disservice to those who have entrusted us to guard and care for their collective collections and the space housing them. The fallout from such debate wracks library management and pits staff against one another. And in the midst of speaking out against phones in the library, the associate director of reference services will feel something buzz in her bluejeans. She'll blush, and go quiet. Then the ringing will begin. It's Missy Elliot this time, 'Gossip Folks,' and *everybody's* got to move: 'Step to me get burnt like toast / Muthafuckas adios amigos / Halves halves, wholes wholes / I don't brag I mostly boast ...' (Elliot, 2002). She's gotta take this one.

No easy answers here, but one technique that may work is to establish and guard (doggedly!) a true quiet study space in the library. Collaboration, conversation, and group work may be fine elsewhere on the floor, but keep one walled-off row of carrels apart, and walk through frequently to hush sneaky talkers. No phones, no talk, no rapping, no wrapping: just quiet, please. With this technique, phones are not pointedly banned from the library, but rather all noise is banned in a set space within the library. This is not so much standing against phones as it is standing up for an area of quiet. The importance of social networks of scholarship, and providing a place for group learners to work has been noted by Beagle (2006: 45–6) and others. The intelligent use of phones and mobile computing can facilitate the success of such groups.

The vigilance required to maintain a true quiet study area, however, cannot be easily overemphasized. The constant patrolling of that space can be daunting, and the crack-down on the slightest noise or talk may well seem too stern to your patrons. The quiet study space, however, will come to be seen by students who need quiet in order to comprehend what they read as one of the most important spaces on campus or in town – no other facility will guarantee them the silence that *they* need to learn.

In an age eager to teach to any number of diverse learning styles, it should not come as such a shock that the old-fashioned quiet reader needs accommodation too, after all. But even Michael Gorman (1998), the former president of the American Library Association seen by so many as a defender of tradition and caution in libraries, implores us to affirm: 'I will make my library a place of color and light' (even if not of ring and buzz) in order to eschew the old aesthetic ethos of the 'liturgical darkness' of the uptight libraries of yester-decade.

People using their phones

Important cultural issues are at work (and at play) in cell phone use, and our libraries are behooved to gain a working knowledge of how phones are regarded and used by our different populations.

For younger patrons who have grown up with phones, the presence of cell phones (and the presence of the sounds and lights of phones, phones ringing, folks interrupting real-world conversations to talk on phones, etc.) is quite acceptable and natural. For immigrant populations who have used phones as important economic tools, a mobile can be much more than a 'phone' – it has been, as mentioned above, a money-maker. When a phone call can bring in a pickup from Buchanan and move 400 kilos of yams from Ghapo to Trade Town, then your phone is about much more than bling. And that is a phone you do not treat as a toy – a phone that a librarian should not want to part a man from, for fear that she might disrespect or insult him by asking him to leave an establishment because of it, or to leave it with some humorless bureaucrat at the circulation station *because she fears he may misuse it in the space she oversees.*

The usability and diversity of phone services will only increase, as will the social integration of phones and their applications in many varied aspects of our interactions with our people and our physical and informational environments. Libraries have an opportunity, a quickly fading opportunity, to leverage mobile life as a platform for library access and service.

Quick Code

Two-dimensional barcodes are gaining ground and usefulness for mobile computing. These barcodes, called QR Code or Quick Code, have been deployed in marketing campaigns, job advertisements, fliers, and public notices in Japan and Korea for some years now (see Figure 5.2 for street uses of QR Code in action). QR Code barcodes are square, with blocks of black and white pixels arranged in such a way that a mobile phone's camera can recognize

Figure 5.2 Nice socks, nice jeans, nice code

Source: Alexis Rondeau (*http://upload.wikimedia.org/wikipedia/commons/8/81/ Japanese_poster_with_QR_codes.jpg*).

them, align them, and pull data from what may seem like random checkers to human eyes. The data then loads as a web page, or a text message, or an image – there are many possibilities. You even see these things on credit card statements and packing slips these days. Look on any given envelope delivered by the Royal Mail or by UPS – you might see it printed on top of the postage mark. Figure 5.3 shows QR Code for the Wikipedia homepage.

Windows Confucius is an attempt by Microsoft Corporation to put QR Code to work for Windows users, but on Microsoft's terms. Instead of Semacode or Kaywa, which are both free and open-source systems, Microsoft has proprietary QR Code scanning and reading software particular to mobile devices running a Windows mobile operating system. Windows Live Barcode, the latest official

Figure 5.3 QR Code for Wikipedia

Source: http://upload.wikimedia.org/wikipedia/commons/c/ce/WikiQRCode.png.

name for the project codenamed 'Confucius,' has an on-again, off-again history since its beta deployment in 2006.

Open QR Code reader systems, like Kaywa and Semacode, have an advantage over Microsoft in that they have been running, and running well, and running openly, for a relatively long time – since June 2006 in Kaywa's case.

But reading QR Code is a tricky bit of business, and factors like the camera quality and the operating system on the mobile phone can make one QR Code reader system work better or worse than another. Will the proprietary OS demand that the QR reader render the code first through a set of Windows protocols? Will zooming in on the QR Code cause an automatic resizing of the Window, or minimize the Window to the taskbar? There is no panacea here either. Learning enough about these issues to offer services to patrons through QR Code interfaces will represent a steep challenge to most librarians.

A push to patrons' phones

Another smart and ready use for mobile computing is the Library Elf application for sending patrons' account status updates to cell phones.

[Library Elf] is an Internet-based tool for keeping track of what's due, overdue and ready for pickup. Users can keep track of one or more library accounts in one place and receive reminders (sometimes called pre-overdue or early notification). Reminders are sent when the user wants it – before items are due (up to seven days advance notice, weekly notice or everyday reminders). (Elf, 2008)

There is also a web-based profile page side for viewing due-date calendars, books on hold, and other useful features. As of summer 2008, Chang Gung University Library in Taiwan, over 800 libraries in the United States, nearly 100 libraries in Canada, nearly 100 in Australia and New Zealand, and about 45 libraries in the United Kingdom were using Library Elf. (For an updated version of which libraries use this service, check this site: *http://www.libraryelf.com/Libraries .aspx.*) This represents many millions of individual library patrons who are using this service. These patrons are now connected to the library through the same device that connects them to their lovers, their business partners, and their parents: a mobile phone.

Texting on mobile phones, of course, has its own culture. There is a grammar to the l337 sp34k running with speed out from under the thumbs of our youth. Any detailed glossary of texting is beyond the abilities of this librarian to create; but there are some basics we ought to know, especially if considering taking reference service a step further into the realm of mobile computing, and other references are well up to the task. (Many good sites provide this service, and even Wikipedia has a decent article on SMS Language as of January 2009.) So, here we go again: txtN represents YA challnG 4 librarians hu chose 2 face ^ 2 d nEdz of mob lib uzers. But that shouldn't slow us down, not one iota.

This talk of embracing mobile phones in libraries all boils down to the library-sanctioned creation of useful graffiti on library materials. It only increases the information density of a library item to let patrons freely, even wildly, plant QR Code on books or in bathroom stalls, to paste them on shelf-ends, and to stick them on the sides of public OPACs. This is information by patrons for other patrons, and communication between patrons. It goes without saying (but I will say it anyway) that patron-initiated communication campaigns using QR Code as a medium (see Figure 5.4 for an idea of what that may look like) will not always be in the interest of the state, the borough, the shire, the county, the parish, the city, the neighborhood, the village, the street, or the library community itself. There will be abuse in the encouragement of QR Code communication just as there has been in listservs and BBS systems and MySpace comments and even good old fashioned pen-and-paper suggestion box forms. But abuse of a medium is no reason, nor has it ever been a good reason, to throw out or block access to that medium full stop.

Be librarians about it, for God's sake.

Figure 5.4   **Books with QR Code**

Source: http://farm1.static.flickr.com/50/128503476_0ab39a19a8_m.jpg.

6

Second Life and other massively multi-user environments

Virtual worlds are informational worlds, and in the world of information, librarians have an unfair advantage over mere slumlords, pimps, and pushers. Or we ought to. But a survey of Second Life, one of the most successful virtual worlds yet, shows librarians to be woefully outnumbered, out-monied, and way, way out-muscled. We are not the victims here – any lack of influence libraries face in virtual worlds is the fault of librarians, ourselves. If Second Life is good for nothing else, it might be good as a model through which we may consider how library marketing, outreach, and programs work in a very busy, very social, and very sex-and-money oriented world; Second Life, like real life, is all of these. If libraries can successfully serve communities inside such a virtual world, we might also learn lessons applicable to growing in our wake-a-day worlds.

Second Life's history is short. Linden Lab created Second Life from earlier virtual reality projects of the late 1990s (called Linden World), and opened it up for public exploration, creation, and consumption in 2003. It has borne a meteoric growth since, vaulting 'The Lindens' into celebrity status and newsmaker circles. Linden Lab is not a publicly traded company, but public interest in making money by way of 'the grid' (see Figure 6.1) of Second Life continues to

Figure 6.1	Second Life grid logo

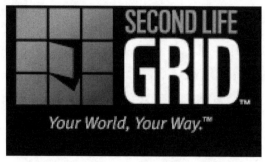

grow; as of May 2008, its annual sales were estimated at 2.8 million US dollars (Sheila Greco, 2008).

Other MMORPGs

Most MMORPGs, MMOGs, or MUDs (massively multiplayer online role-playing games, massively multiplayer online games, and multi-user dungeons, that is) are used for gaming. Even though Second Life is seen by many as a game, it isn't. Second Life is different because it is a whole environment, a virtual world with no particular globally mandated content-oriented agendas. It doesn't take many steps backwards from a grid like Second Life to the old multi-user dungeons, which are text-based, all the way to choose-your-own-adventure books (which *were* sort of globally mandated content-oriented narrative agendas). We shouldn't forget that reading, for that matter, is also an immersive virtual reality experience.

I remember playing an early text-based MUD. I must have been seven or eight years old. A friend would run into the classroom after recess (where I'd be writing steadily on my multiplication tables for punishment work) and invite me down to the 'gifted kids' center where he took classes. There was the gray Formica table, with two Tandy machines (TRS-80s, I think – after the Commodore PET and before the Tandy 1000s, anyway). I would sit at the old green-and-black monochrome, sticky with coconut candy from the last kid who got permission to play, clicking tightly sprung keys, and typing something from my brief suite of remembered commands: look around; turn right; talk; pick up; open door. If the command worked, I'd get an interaction with a computer automated non-player character: *The troll laughs deeply and lifts his mace.* If I got it wrong, some smarmy comment would pop up: *There's no door to open there; you're staring at the cave wall; talk to whom?* The green cursor blinked, and blinked, and blinked. That tiny exchange, the field of BASIC black and flickering green letters, was enough to open up whole worlds in my imagination (see Figure 6.2 if you're not

Figure 6.2   Will Crowther's MUD from 1984

```
PAUSE   INIT DONE statement executed
To resume execution, type go.  Other input will terminate the job.
go
Execution resumes after PAUSE.
WELCOME TO ADVENTURE!!  WOULD YOU LIKE INSTRUCTIONS?


SOMEWHERE NEARBY IS COLOSSAL CAVE, WHERE OTHERS HAVE FOUND
FORTUNES IN TREASURE AND GOLD, THOUGH IT IS RUMORED
THAT SOME WHO ENTER ARE NEVER SEEN AGAIN. MAGIC IS SAID
TO WORK IN THE CAVE.  I WILL BE YOUR EYES AND HANDS. DIRECT
ME WITH COMMANDS OF 1 OR 2 WORDS.
(ERRORS, SUGGESTIONS, COMPLAINTS TO CROWTHER)
(IF STUCK TYPE HELP FOR SOME HINTS)


YOU ARE STANDING AT THE END OF A ROAD BEFORE A SMALL BRICK
BUILDING . AROUND YOU IS A FOREST. A SMALL
STREAM FLOWS OUT OF THE BUILDING AND DOWN A GULLY.
```

Source: http://upload.wikimedia.org/wikipedia/en/3/35/ADVENT_-_Will_
      Crowther's_original_version.png.

picturing this yet). From it, I spun stories based on my little adventures there, and made up my own takes on the tales of warring wizards and Machiavellian feudal turf wars. The computer screen would lead me and my friends to run around in the woods, fencing with young pine limbs and diving into green ditches to dodge dragon's breath. How is that possible?

Games and their worlds

There are very few MUDs or virtual environments that are not primarily oriented to particular games or built around a game world. That is to say, most virtual worlds are not meta-worlds – they exist within a particular genre and with finite rules and dimensions that may be based on a novel, previous game, or movie. They've got those globally mandated content-oriented agendas at work. EverQuest and World of Warcraft are extremely popular virtual worlds, with World of Warcraft alone having over 10 million subscribers globally (Alexander, 2008), and each have genres that overarch and dictate the types of stories that can be told or played within their worlds.

The Sims Online (going through a change into 'EA-Land' as of this writing) was an example of a virtual world built around a video game that originally existed only on console and computer. Despite its firm couching within the Sims brand and milieu, there exists many dramatic points of crossover and even intrigue between The Sims Online and Second Life. The activities of the media within The Sims Online, for example, and the political fallout of its activities in that world (and in Second Life and real life) demonstrates the very real effects of people who are not just playing in these worlds, but are living in such a way that uses the avatar as a tool to effect wider change (Ludlow, 2007). People seek information, fight for principles, hunt for cheap thrills, ambush others, steal, seek sex, and rally for causes in these worlds. In effect, people do (or try to do) whatever they might like to try in real life. If it were just a game, all of these activities would be pointed toward accomplishing finite tasks to win gold, merit, points, money, or gear; but this is clearly not the case. These 'gamers' often accomplish their most interesting and influential feats by doing what they really love or are really interested in, regardless of what in-game or in-world glory or fortune it may or may not bring them. I am, unfortunately, thinking now of an apparent-goblin with a phallus affixed to its brow who went leaping through the public lecture spaces of the Second Life Library courtyard one afternoon. This act was seemingly one of its own creative exuberance, with no connection to rewards either in-world or out.

We could say that many or most of these virtual environments are environments for infinite games, in the James P. Carse sense of the term (Carse, 1987). These are spaces to play (and live, and work) in ways that perpetuate the play (and life, and economy). 'Finite games are played to be won, but infinite games are games that you play in order to continue playing,' as Carse says. The world is full of both kinds of games. Libraries are great examples of both types of 'games' being played simultaneously by patrons, librarians, and administrators. The infinite game of collection development, improved information literacy for the community, and the refinement of finding aids and subject guides, serve as the backdrop to finite games of locating particular books on the shelves, finding statistics in databases, and collecting fines for overdue materials. These models, finite and infinite, work well as lenses through which we might see more and learn more about virtual worlds, too.

The Sims, and all its variations both online and in stand-alone console format, is one of the most popular virtual worlds ever, selling over 6.3 million copies in its first two years of existence. The Sims is in some ways an infinite game, where much of the play surrounds dressing your character, interacting with other characters, and sustaining your character's position among others and the routine of her daily life; but in some ways it is itself a finite game, because the overall structure of play leads players to increase connections, improve the quality of their interactions with others, and take care of themselves (through routines like washing and eating) so that they might advance into positions of more power, wealth, and skill.

A world like RuneScape (see Figures 6.3 and 6.4) is a world full of finite games, and a set of accomplishable tasks that advance your character's status. One finds a pirate or makes a deal with a wizard to gain higher rank and more abilities. RuneScape seen on a macro-level, however, is an infinite game because there is not a point at which, or a set of steps one may take in order to, 'win RuneScape.' RuneScape evolves as you play, and you might play for years and years. I started a RuneScape account in 2006, completed a quest or two, and still log in occasionally years later to try new things with the avatar.

RuneScape is also an interesting space in that it has tried to fashion itself as an educational tool; the Varrock Museum, for

Figure 6.3 RuneScape is an extremely popular world

Source: Jagex, Inc. (*http://www.jagex.com/img/corporate/images/press/logos/ PressLogo_RunescapeHD_Mn.jpg*).

Figure 6.4　RuneScape server locations map

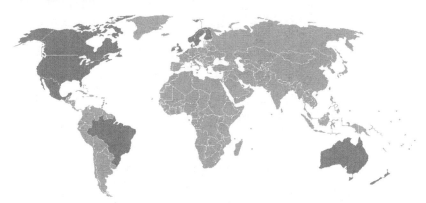

Source: Coasttocoast & CaptainVindaloo (*http://upload.wikimedia.org/ wikipedia/commons/2/2b/RuneScape_server_location_map.png*).

example, exists explicitly to tell the history of RuneScape (which, in turn, requires that participants make up that history). It appeals mainly to children and teenagers, is strictly policed to prevent abusive behavior between players, and is easily accessible in most schools and public libraries via its website (RuneScape.com). Jagex, the company that created and maintains RuneScape, overtly attempts to use their platform to educate players, to create scenarios that encourage the development of skills to help in daily life, and to challenge players with puzzles that encourage thinking; all of this lends itself with little difficulty to library game days and tournaments (McGowan, 2007; Phillips, 2006). The finite tasks that Jagex and others hold out as educational are problematic, however. If the argument for RuneScape as an educational space hinges on developing skills that help us daily, we must ask: (1) how many kids chop down trees, mine for ore, or bury chicken bones daily, and (2) how is performing these tasks in RuneScape supposed to help them learn to perform those skills in real life? The question of whether and to what degree performing virtual demonstrations of activities may help one to learn and acquire real skill, we must leave to experts in pedagogy and psychology. The question, however, of what use it may be to learn how to mine for ore or bury chicken bones generally (to whatever degree of expertise we may learn it), we can leave quite safely to the realm of common sense.

Kozierok (2007), while acknowledging that RuneScape does include some positive educational elements, says that players 'also get a broad education in the negative aspects of online gaming, including cheating, scamming, lying, taunting, bullying, gambling, and addiction.' RuneScape is not an age restricted space (as Second Life's Teen Grid is), so we end up with eight-year-olds playing alongside forty-year-olds, and with the ease of modifying (read: lying about) online personas and real identities, RuneScape has the potential to become a natural sink for malicious, deceitful, or just plain slimy people to go hangout with and pick on kids.

Crowe (2006), however, suggests the average age of RuneScape players is 16. The social space they discover in RuneScape turns out to be by far the most important element of the world; educational activities and success in the game(s) are found to be not nearly as important as relaxing and spending time with friends, reinforcing social norms, and discovering how other players relate to and interact with your peer group. Worries of abuse may therefore be overblown, as 'the kids' themselves watch out for each other and run off in-world annoyances; Axegrrl did just that with the pestering merchant trying to sell lobsters to her and her mates as they were relaxing by Braxton Waterfall (Crowe, 2006).

Second Life Library

Since 2006, Second Life has had its own public library. Starting out as 'Second Life Library,' the Alliance Library System's own information service, complete with real estate to build on, volunteer staff, and a busy schedule of author appearances, is now located on an archipelago of islands branching off from the original Info Island. In the system there is now HealthInfo Island, and, on the Teen Grid, Land of Lincoln.

There is an information hub already built into the structure of Second Life, and that way station is the default home location of all avatars. It is there, at this start-spot, that you can get general information on Second Life, experiment with movement and flight, and get tutorials on many aspects of life in Second Life. It also serves as a major information hub for both in-world news and bits and pieces from the congregated avatars' real-life lives. People talk, and smart visitors listen; but the information hub is by no means a library.

Over the course of Second Life Library's existence, I have often wondered (and sometimes publicly questioned, both online and at conferences) *how does this help my patrons tonight, when they come asking for help at the reference desk?*

Good answers are rare and pricey, it seems. I've had folks try to dodge or spin this question way more often than attempt a direct answer. From passing bloggers to affiliates of Alliance Library System itself, no one has ever admitted, either, that real-life applications of Second Life for helping our information-seeking communities are scarce and dubious. As Spencer Smith, a Texan librarian, put it (2008) when asked how Second Life helps patrons:

> The answer is, 'It doesn't help your patrons at all ... especially considering the amazingly low percentage of your patrons that participate in Second Life at all.'
> Basically, this is an excuse for librarians to play games online while pretending to do something job-related. No one complains, because then it will be taken away and they'll have to find something else to do instead of doing their jobs.

Smith makes a fair point – the allure of using time to explore a glamorous and dynamic virtual cybertopia (a seemingly good fit for libraries, anyway) is hard to deny, especially when there is the promise, however faint and slender, that such exploration *now* may lead to larger benefits *later*. Having mapped it out, written scripts, and made connections well ahead of time, Librarian Z will be best suited to lead the way and bring the unenthused into Second Life a little less painfully when the order comes from the dean or director that *it's high time we stake our claim in-world!*

I *have* learned from Second Life evangelists that building a library in Second Life is *great* for *institutional marketing*. It is also very useful indeed, it turns out, for a great-big-gigantic four-dimensional game of Barbie dress-up. So.

The question remains: How do our patrons benefit from library services in Second Life?

Well, firstly, it is not normally *our patrons* as we may have traditionally defined or identified them, who benefit. But that is not to say patrons do not benefit. We just don't know who it is that we are helping in Second Life when someone comes up to the reference desk – and that is fine, because in the public library model at work in the United States, Great Britain, Europe and, indeed, most of the rest of the world for the last hundred years or so, we help any and all who ask for it. (This is of course, to gloss over the sick history of racial segregation and elitism built into Victorian ideas about who should and who has the right to read in the first place.) But we help any and all. We do not check your identity to ensure that you are 'one of us,' or a taxpayer, or even a national. We just help you, *because that's the library way.* That's what librarians do.

So why not follow that very same model and reach out into virtual service with arms open to anonymous avatars?

Mainly because we are supported, by and large, on public funds provided by our locals. Our communities, in a very bricks-and-mortar sense, in a very hedgerow and local pizza dive sense, support us. If we invest man-hours, energy, time, brain power, and computer resources into a reference service, that reference service should serve (primarily!) the community who provided the resources that got the service built in the first place. Service in Second Life serves one of the 13 million wandering avatars who happen through the doors and up to the desk. The avatar might be ridden by a kid in Saskatoon or a granny in Calais – or maybe even by the plumber who lives down the lane. But the service provided in Second Life is global. When locals pay for service, that service ought to primarily serve the locals unless the locals want it otherwise.

Zygmunt Bauman got some deserved buzz in the late 1990s for his take on globalization, and it deserves some play here, in terms of libraries. Bauman, a venerable sociologist at the University of Leeds, put his take on the tensions between global and local forces in terms of commerce, travel, communication, and other dimensions. He threw new light on the means of the powerful to move through space on their own terms. Partly framed as a study of disparity between 'globals and locals' (1998: 7–29, 85–9), his view of the 'local' person was of one who was stuck spatially, having to settle for the circumstances of places he couldn't leave – but also having the luxury of time to explore said place and live in it fully. This quantity of time, though enforced by an inability to escape the bounded space, was time which a global person lacked. On the other hand, though he may have little or no time to enjoy it, the global is so free of place and the physicality of space that he may enter a sort of 'cyberspatial heaven' in which bodies don't even really matter anymore (1998: 19–20).

Bauman's views on globalization are relevant here – it is the 'global person' who may enjoy virtual realms like Second

Life. Even if a patron is very locally bound, and comes into the library to enjoy the free computer lab, it is only thanks to a global system of infrastructure built thanks to great riches provided by the labor of locals all over the world that she can do so at all. Well, when does she stop being local and begin being a global? When does the yam farmer on his mobile phone, outside of Shongolo, Mississippi, become a global? I think this question of distinction matters, though it is not a question I can answer here.

There are, no doubt, many benefits to serving a global community for both those served and for the library doing the serving. Many of our services here in the late nought-noughts are already global and do already reach non-local patrons. Virtual reference service through e-mail, instant messaging, phone texting (or, for that matter, contact through Second Life), often make no differentiation between patrons who e-mail from down the road or from across international shipping lanes. Good librarians give it their best each and every time, and that is as it should be; just as we don't ask for proof of citizenship upon admitting entrance into our stacks, we should not *in principle* turn queriers away because they cannot provide proof of locality.

This becomes, after a time, a civic or political issue – and not an abstract one – to be sorted out by library administrators alongside city, county, shire or university big hats. Can locals afford to serve the globals? Librarians may have to weigh in on these policy decisions, and Second Life, that slick not-a-game that sexes up reference service in the eyes of so many, will be a proving ground for local library service policies.

If your vicar feels snubbed at the reference desk you've got a problem. If the vicar feels snubbed *and* your reference librarians have snubbed her because they are busy helping goth-dinosaur-elf-vampire-cyborgs find great in-world sources for real (virtual) estate value fluctuations near Electric-Lust Island, then you've got a really *big* problem. (No categorical offense meant to goth-dinosaur-elves, or to their friends or lovers. In fact, respect is due for innovating on that under-appreciated personality genre.)

Real life demands real presence, real attention. Good old eye contact, a simple smile or nod of acknowledgement, and a willingness to drop what you are working on as soon as possible in order to dive into a reference request: nothing beats that. Nothing builds trust between you and your patrons like that. If you mark the book you were working with, stand and listen, then search the catalog with your patron, teaching how it's done as you go, and take him into the stacks to find the source he needs, and if you do it earnestly and as patiently as possible, then you have created a loyal patron who has reason to trust you. If any of that gets interrupted, anywhere along the way by laziness, apathy, smarminess, or disinterest, you may be setting up an atmosphere of antipathy between your library and the community it serves. Add in a dash of (what will be seen as) playing dress-up in a computer world, and your patrons may even feel betrayed. You will have chosen a fantasy in a plastic box over their very real, immediate, and intimate human need to find and know.

These stakes are big, and trust is not easy to rebuild. Sometimes it even takes elaborate remarketing and rebranding campaigns in which the library is reimagined by its community after considerable and costly change to make things right again with those you serve. These matters of trust are decided daily, moment by moment, with each interaction we have with our patrons.

Yes, virtual patrons matter too – after all, the 'virtual' patron could be the chair-bound Asperger's kid that lives down by the warehouse, half a mile from the library. Finding the properly struck balance between service to all and service to the one in front of you is only made more difficult by the many new and quickly changing means to communicate. Second Life, again, will be the grounds that act as the front lines on which we work at sorting these issues out. There has never before been such a popular, easy to use, and potentially useful immersive virtual environment, and it is clearly a very fertile area for conflict (and cooperation) between locals and globals.

On a practical note, you can begin your mitigation of real-life patron recoil by simply not serving patrons in Second Life while you are manning the reference or circulation areas of your library. If promotion and development of in-world service is something that your library thinks needs pursuing, by all means do so; but do so in workroom offices or in a workspace away from immediate public view. If Second Life is not on display while patrons struggle with the bricks-and-mortar search for, evaluation of, and implementation of information sources, there will not be any complaints about the reference librarian snubbing the vicar in favor of the goth-dinosaur-whatsits. That is an easy way to avoid the conflict before there even is a conflict at all.

Librarians as virtual escorts

Another method for bringing your real-life community along with you on Second Life service is, well, to really bring them into Second Life. Offer a series of classes on building avatars, moving and flight, in-world communication and mapping, and building goods and places. Your community might just get interested enough to build a Second Life mirror of their own favorite local shops and churches. You get a group of farmers near Keele village at work to build a 'Second Keele' in-world, and soon they may be using virtual modeling techniques to teach about local produce, sustainable agriculture in the Midlands, and even marketing their farms to buyers in-world for real sales to real grocery stores in real life in Newcastle-under-Lyme. In no time, the produce manager down at the Sainsbury's has got a new source for aubergines. Why not?

Maybe it's like Warren Ellis said in one of his Second Life pieces for Reuters ('Shipwrecked and abandoned'):

> Lots of people have had lots to say about the recent hype surrounding Second Life, but very few have addressed the basic experience of the world – that you're incredibly alone there. You can spend eighty percent of your time walking through immense, labyrinthine castles that no one lives in. Visit a seemingly endless string of shops with no customers.

The public library of Second Life, thanks to the Alliance folks and many volunteers, works its heart out to address that very issue, to build community and bring people *in world* together. If it is having any effect at all, maybe it's all worth it after all. Go walk and fly in Second Life awhile. Go build a weird, wet autopoietic art-device. Go chat with a feathered stranger under a glowing orange milkshake. Go decide for yourself.

Learn French

The 'cool space' and leisure aspect of these environments bring up some very interesting issues for librarians. If EA-Land or RuneScape is mainly visited and used by people who just want to explore, relax, and have fun (as in Figure 6.5), then librarians have to carefully think about the kinds of roles they

Figure 6.5   Ecole SL (French school)

Source: Ecole-sl.com (*http://s3.amazonaws.com/sl_showcase/_venue/978.jpg*).

wish to perform in these spaces. If libraries are seen as places to work rather than places to hang out, then librarians may not be welcome in RuneScape. Try as hard as you like, if you bring books and studies to Braxton Waterfall, Axegrrl will probably axe you. Should she see you and your institution as an innovative and outreaching bastion of enlightenment? Maybe so, but if you interrupt her chill time it doesn't much matter. If she needs to study, she'll find her way to you.

Imagine you wear your nice little pastel pantsuit, take a briefcase and laptop computer, a short stack of reference books under your left arm, and march yourself right up into the midst of a crowded food-court at a busy mall on Friday evening. How many teens would see your presence as an 'innovation in library service'? Many would see your well-preened and prudish presence as an intrusion into their time for relaxing, hanging out with mates, and making fun of old people. You might end up having to pick the chips off your pink lapels. More likely, though, you would just be ignored. We see lots of libraries just being ignored on Web 2.0.

Not everything has to be explicitly about education. And not all library programs need to relate directly to classic works of literature or the patterns of formal logic. Some spaces just are not meant for libraries or librarians – there are some spaces which we should leave well enough alone. But there is another aspect of this, which brings us to what I see as a minor tributary to this discussion (other librarians will protest the 'minorness' of it): libraries themselves can become fun spaces, hangout spaces, chill rooms, even game rooms, that are not academically oriented. Libraries can be media centers for discovering information, playing games, and connecting with peers through formats including magazines, mp3s, and Play Station 3 controllers. So, it may be that libraries do have a stake in (and a right to exist in) virtual worlds geared toward fun and leisure. However, knowing when to stay out of the roller rink and the pub is just as important as knowing when to make library spaces more game-room and pub-like.

Most of us, though, will be thinking about what services we might offer when we're considering a move into a virtual world. If it is to be a reference service that you want to deliver, if it is information literacy tutoring or reader's advisory you want to work at in an online world, do so in a world appropriate for it. Second Life is probably your best bet for these (rather than EA-Land, for example; see Figure 6.6 for a view of Info Island).

Lori Bell (see Appendix 1) talks about the whole virtual environment as a medium; immersed in a four-dimensional virtual world, we are apprehending and using information in ways far removed from scanning an e-mail or watching a video. In this way, a virtual world becomes a set of models for things we might wish to learn more about or to create from scratch. A good virtual world is a meta-model and a medium in itself. In discussing who may become providers

Figure 6.6   Learning Space on Info Island

of virtual spaces, Castronova (2005) makes a case for non-profit agencies, educational organizations, and even governmental actors to build new virtual models as teaching and testing devices. Although he never uses libraries as an example of what might be done, and who might do it, he points out that opportunities for *doing* things (not just teaching or showing models of things) are plentiful in virtual worlds; this is something libraries can press to their advantage. In discussing gender discrimination, he leads off into an important point about the creation of the kinds of worlds we want to live in, or just test out:

> Want a world that surrounds visitors in your religious views? You can build it. Concerned that a disadvantaged group does not have access to a Very Good Thing? Make a world where everyone can get that thing for free. Have a hope for a different future if some policy were to

change? Build that future. If you can craft a social world that people like, you have just made a powerful argument for the policy decisions and cultural attitudes implicit in the world's design. (Castronova, 2005: 142)

What about modeling a Sim City very similar to your own, in which the referendum for the new nuclear power plant is passed and the plant gets built? You mean my library can do that? And we can walk around in the Metro Town of tomorrow, poking and prodding at the pros and cons of nuclear energy? And inside the model, there is pervasive – nay, ubiquitous! – information items linking visitors to local, state, and federal laws, environmental and safety statistics, past energy policies, and links to the records of contractors who are vying to build the nuclear plant? That's impressive librarianship! And, look, there flies a flock of geese.

If your patrons become invested in a virtual world, they may become as interested, territorial, defensive, and consumed by it as they become with blogs, or their laptops, or their own homes.

Wagner James Au writes about the war (or battle, at least) that broke out in Second Life on the birthday of Martin Luther King Jr, 2007, when tensions between the anti-immigrant French political party *Front National* and its neighbors in-world finally boiled over. *Front National* had bought space in a popular urban area of Second Life, and, though they had done nothing overtly aggressive in-world up to that time, their presence (and, quite probably, their known potential for intolerance and initiating violence against their neighbors in real life) disturbed a segment of the population. Au relates how one protester-turned-combatant flippantly responded to questions about the paradox of using violence to defeat a violent enemy with 'I don't know ... I don't care,' and then returned to his attack, 'unleashing another barrage. Another innovative insurrectionist created pig grenades, fixed them to a flying saucer, and sent several whirling into *Front National* headquarters, where they'd explode in a starburst of porcine shrapnel' (Au, 2008: 185).

The 'so what?' of a virtual war that does no damage to the inhabitants or properties is not lost on Au, but he uses the episode to underline the psychological and political (and perhaps even legal) importance of virtual worlds, and the groups that meet, work, and play there. When an intolerant political party sets up camp in a virtual space that patrons visit much more often than any physical spaces where the party may headquarter in real life, they 'feel intruded upon, feel invaded, feel as if this hate is no longer an odd abstraction somewhere out there in the unaccountable anonymity of the Internet,' or, perhaps, in the unaccountable anonymity of bureaucracies, menu trees, call-backs, e-mail forms, automated operators, and red tape that normally separates citizens from real political process and interaction (Au, 2008: 187).

A great library director (Pamela Pridgen of Hattiesburg, Mississippi) once told me that once you offer a service, you'd better not take it away. That was in reference to a cumbersome fax machine we offered for public use in the Reference Department. Folks had come to rely on being able to fax documents for just a couple of dollars, though we in the reference department sometimes found it difficult to juggle faxing from a side room and keeping an eye on the reference desk simultaneously. She could see clearly that our library was the only ready point-of-fax between downtown and the state highway (a span of several miles), and that taking the service away, no matter how much of a pain it might be for us, was not in the community's interest. The lesson applies here, too, and online – once you offer advanced web search classes in Second Life, or build an open-air garden of religious tolerance where patrons can stroll and read and rest (as Alliance Library System has done), or citizenship tutorials for immigrants, or whatever service or space you may offer that comes to be loved and well-used by your community, you are going to cause soreness if you try to take it away, or if you let it fall into poor quality. If a virtual service becomes so important that your library decides to build and maintain immersive structures and systems, rest assured – your patrons will become invested in it, in any number of dimensions, including the emotional.

That nuclear energy plant in Metro Town? Imagine rewriting the space in some unfair and politically biased way just before voting day – imagine the reactions of the voters and their representatives as they stroll through a virtual Metro Town, post meltdown. Heaped piles of black slag half-bury livestock, houses, and pregnant women; a goose lays flapping, spinning itself in slow circles with its one good wing, honking a slurry dirge as pinpricks of bright pink fallout dot the gray sky and drift, like fairytale hexes, to the earth as warm ash. The protest would be much more than virtual, and the ramifications would be much more serious than a mere denial-of-service attack.

Even played straight, no table-tilting meta-narrative management involved, Metro Town might become the site of protests and counterprotests in-world, as various competing interests try so hard to demonstrate the good (see the well-groomed executives with floating slides of serene, green hills, rolling away toward the Lake District touting The Nuclear Choice, The Environmental Choice: The Smart Choice for England!) and the bad (see the mothers clutching children close to their skirts, shooting arcs of words dripping blood through the virtual sky: Chernobyl, Mutation, Radiation, Poison ...), and both with a great and zealous fervor.

Patrons invest in their places, and in-world is an increasingly important place. What role will your library play in these new tensions?

7

Arphids: promise and dangers

Arphids do not yet do enough for us to worry widely about what they are doing, in a daily way, in our stacks – but they soon will. Radio Frequency Identification tags (RFID, or arphid as writer Bruce Sterling calls upon us to call them when we mean 'RFID as social or art object') simply send a serial number to a database when it gets hit with a specific frequency of radiowave. That interaction between database, serial number, and tag forms an interactive loop that ties information about an object's identity to the arphid attached (or tagged) to said object.

Memory in these RFID tags is getting better, and the tags themselves are getting cheaper (soon to near the marketing singularity of less than 0.03 Euros per tag). It is possible, then, that arphids may soon come to contain the databases they have only pinged in the past; the geolocative hardware and the context-rich, identity-granting software become both at once more generally distributed and more pointedly local.

Some technical specifications and facts about RFID would serve us well, from the time before they were 'arphids.' RFID has existed since the early-to-mid twentieth century in some form (there is debate about which of the predecessors of RFID actually constitute the first true identification system, so the date of origin varies), but formal rules for its implementation have only lately begun to be systematically created and agreed upon by corporations and governments. In 1999 a European Union directive regulated RFID use in the United Kingdom, although it has fallen to individual EU members to enforce the rules (Fregoso, 2007: 439). The antenna in the Radio Frequency Identification tag responds to radio signals from an outside source (in the case of 'passive' tags) by producing a corresponding signal. When that response signal is recognized by the RFID reader, information is exchanged. To reproduce the excellent explanation in Merk et al.'s *Pervasive Computing Handbook*:

> [Passive tags] do not require a power supply – they obtain the necessary energy from the radio frequency field emitted by the reader device. An RF antenna captures the radio frequency energy to appropriate voltage levels for chip operation. Data is superimposed on the carrier wave so communication to and from the chip uses the same antenna as the power supply. (Merk et al., 2001: 63)

Active tags carry their own power source, usually a battery (though innovations in solar power have led to active solar tags and other power sources, such as body heat, are on the horizon now), and can speak without first being spoken to, if you will. These tags emit radio bursts autonomously, usually in an 'always on' mode. If an RFID reader is nearby, it will pick up the signal from the active tag and register the serial number.

So should we be worried – see Figure 7.1?

Figure 7.1 Stop RFID?

Source: http://upload.wikimedia.org/wikipedia/commons/2/22/Stoprfid-logo.jpg.

Smart tags on smart books

RFID tags currently have what seems like very small memories, especially when compared with other 'remembering devices' we may be used to, like e-mail accounts, flash drives, or iPods. We talk about hundreds of megabytes, or gigabytes for data exchanged with iPhones. My gmail account currently gives me 6.8 gigabytes of storage – which I can use for a lot more than e-mails. Yahoo! Mail gives me unlimited storage. The flash drive in my pocket (an itty-bitty Creative Zen Nano mp3 player) gives me 512 megabytes. Compare that to your typical RFID tag, which usually has a memory of only up to a few hundred bytes. With such limited memories, the RFID can currently only be used as a simple index, shouting a string of numbers whenever it is called to do so by its complementary RFID reader. In 2001, the data capacity of smart labels ranged 'from 64 to 2K bits ... the smallest-capacity and simplest smart labels have a single, factory-programmed data block containing a unique serial number,' and, for most of these

109

labels or tags, that data is locked and unmodifiable (Hansmann, 2003: 65). These are simple beasties. They just bark and bark back at each other.

But even at the turn of the century, more complex and elaborate RFID tags were in development, and that development is trending upwards quickly. Hansmann notes that some tags, even in 2001, had memories that could be both read and written to, as well as partitioned into multiple blocks for different reasons. Password keys are in play to unlock particular blocks on the tag, and even a hint of larger internal memories for expanded data storage were in development (65). Six years later, Sam Liu (2007) writes of Boeing's use of an Intelleflex RFID smart tag that has 64 kilobytes of onboard memory *for each RFID tag*. As Liu says, 'Extended memory enables these tags to operate as portable databases to deliver real-time, actionable information without the need for network connectivity.' The network is set now to disappear into the object.

The possibility emerges for everything to become tagged, for arphids to be integrated, along with the information that makes them useful, into everything. 'All of your books' is a subset, by the way, of 'everything.' The ubiquity of tagged objects will heighten the need people will have for our skills as librarians. Information sorting, parsing the ads and misinformation from useful stuff (perhaps even down to the line-by-line level) is something that information professionals are increasingly called to do as the general public becomes overwhelmed by the scale of information management they must face in daily life. That means that when arphids hit the hardest, they will hit a body of library patrons in all nations that have already become generally sloppy with information management practices. (Why fact-check or evaluate your sources? A quick and shallow stab at Googling seems good enough for most of our patrons.) Too many believe that if it is written (in print or on the Web) it must be true, or at least legitimate. Librarians, more than most, have a duty to start thinking about the information practices and habits that may grow out of this geolocative technology; we must start thinking about the coming impact of arphids now because quite soon we will be in a position to stand ready to mitigate the damage and help manage all of that information for the communities we serve.

Let's stop now and think about what will happen when our books become 'blogjects,' constantly updating and appending themselves, constantly informing us and our patrons of each object's activity, location, and current use and user. As our patrons become reliant on the accuracy of the information from their lorries (telling them when they need service and where to find the nearest petrol station) and their trainers (telling them how far they have walked, and how many steps are left to their favorite pub), consider your new role in a library collection enabled with arphids pushing incorrect or unauthoritative news or ads to other books, phones, blogs, laptops, magazines, and Bebo profiles. A talkative book makes for a very dynamic collection. Boiling this down, even, to a simple two-body problem of print-book communicating with an electronic version of itself, myriad issues arise.

First consider whether the e-book in question is local. It is important to confirm whether it is stored on a local database, establishing a unique local copy, or whether all changes reflected in the e-book become visible universally, for all viewers of the book, everywhere. Librarians, in many cases, will wish to lean toward local copies of e-books – even if the 'local' copy is stored on a server in Mountain View, California, our patrons will need to append, amend, and 'write in the margins' of the e-book in such a way that does not bar others in other libraries from making notations in their own copies of the same e-title. If the e-book is truly open and universally accessible, then the model begins to look much more like a wiki, or perhaps a so-called 'wikibook' with only the main body of text locked to changes. When dealing with the specific needs of a specific group of patrons, however, a 'closed wiki' model, at least, would be of much better service; if millions of users add marginalia to an atlas of Mississippi's Piney Woods region, it will not help the farmers near Lumberton much in designating where the borders of DeSoto National Forest run, or in tracking a herd of whitetail deer in the frost pocket near the Dana Farm. Specific communities need community-specific information, and the access question for the e-books becomes a very important one.

This tension is heightened by the relationships between an e-book (whether local or catholic) and its corresponding local print version. An arphid-enabled print book has a very special and precarious relationship to the e-book. The print version is not made obsolete by the e-book; indeed, the e-book can gain much value from the print book. Figure 7.2 shows a close-up of a typical library RFID tag. The print book can log who uses

Figure 7.2   Examples of RFID barcodes

Source: *http://upload.wikimedia.org/wikipedia/commons/b/b9/RFID-stick.jpg.*

it (to the degree that the person using it wishes to reveal her identity), for how long, and for what. This is very useful information for marketing, and for determining things like use-hours and wear for physical materials, circulation trends, and collection development needs. The print book can log information about which other books it is used with or alongside, and for how long. This data is useful for finding subject-area interconnections, which may later be exploited by canny librarians looking to cook up clever new programs for outreach and instruction. The print book can direct patrons to the e-book version (and all related online content, discussion, and links), thereby driving up the usage statistics of the e-book.

And the e-book can, in turn, deliver much to the print copy. For example, a local e-book might give patrons a space to scrawl in on the 'back cover,' and in this way they can leave notes to each other about the physical collection. (*If you need a good, simple colour mix chart, see John Barber's book – one shelf over to the left, 751.422. The text is torn out of the first chapter, and somebody's spilled coffee on the cover, but the mixing charts are still there, and in great shape!*) The e-book can give a venue for an online forum directed back at the physical collection, which is context, collection, and community specific.

E-books and traditional print books may merge through arphids, kirkyan-style (just Google 'kirkyan' to read more about Sven Johnson's design thought experiment), into a new type of format altogether. This would make complaints about the clunkiness of e-book 'readers' (see Herring, 2005) obsolete. E-books are so far best accessed on the Web, in a web browser. Mobile browsers still have some growing and developing to do, but open, web-based formats so far outshine the proprietary and DRM-ridden models like Amazon's Kindle. Either way, e-books and print books, bridged by arphids, become something else altogether. Not quite a website, not quite a 'book,' but something more akin to an open blog travelogueing the release of a new album: the people use it, and by using it they make the contents their own.

Neil Gershenfeld summarizes his take on the problems of bits meeting books with an appeal to see this as a both/and rather than an either/or situation:

> Choosing between books and computers makes as much sense as choosing between breathing and eating. Books do a magnificent job of conveying static information; computers let information change. We're just now learning how to use a lot of new technology to match the performance of the mature technology in books, trascending inherent limits without sacrificing its best features. The bits and the atoms belong together. The story of the book is not coming to an end; it's really just beginning. (Gershenfeld, 1999).

Arphids in the collection reminds us that there is no longer a meaningful difference between virtual, augmented, or 'real' because real has become infused with what was once virtual. Perhaps it is the case that any metaphysical qualities of difference between virtual reality and real reality are false: all real experience is experienced reality, whether mediated by machines or not. The differences and alliances between real books and their electronic versions (which are clearly more than mere copies) take us several steps beyond this idea. Without its Benjamin-ian aura, a book becomes an open system, including its readers in new ways to produce new meta-content and behoove new avenues of discussion between readers and readers, books and readers, and books and books (authors are in there somewhere, too).

Arphids help with all of this. Arphids are one mechanization by which the emancipation of the book from its parasitical dependence on ritual setting, to borrow a line, might occur; or, to an ever greater degree, the book as mediated and modified by its e-versions becomes the book better designed for use, re-use, reproducibility (Benjamin, 1936). It becomes the book it was always meant to be, unfettered now but still strengthened by its place in space and time, its physical binding, and the mechanics of the bit of circuitry belching radio frequencies from board and spine to machine and network.

We must continue to loudly champion good search techniques and information evaluation skills; suddenly our suggestions for better research practices become must-know skills – the basic business of twenty-first century 'life literacy.' All of this points toward a practice of preparation for a totally new type of debate about keeping library spaces quiet. The books and machines and people, no longer so separate, need help in navigating the borders between themselves, between advertisements and government documents, between information that is asked for and information that is not. We will be shushing our spaces for a long time to come – but we will no longer shush the patrons so much as the shouty third-party applications riding rough on the backs of their mobile phones, infecting books and blogs and online eyeglasses with abandon.

There is a new wave of personal, hyperlocal, and space/time contextual advertising about to bear down on our patrons. Our job is to make sure they have the information-literacy and critical thinking skills necessary to make sense of it and make use of it. The old themes rise again: accuracy, authority, currency, objectivity, and scope of the information – advocating for patrons by teaching these skills is our new duty. The old skills of matching content to authority headings or the alphabetization of back issues gives way to post-arphid duties: teaching our patrons personal information self-defense. Arphids will not relent in spamming our patrons or their personal information management gizmos – computers, phones, or whatever comes next, and that is too big an opportunity for the trained information professionals in the world's libraries to overlook.

Hacking, playing, and phreaking out: is this real-world or exercise? Over?

Now is the time for librarians to begin 'wargame' exercises for arphid scenarios.

In wargaming, the aim is to model a situation in which you can try to break things on purpose to find out where the faults are. Trust is necessary among library staff in wargaming. It will not do to have a circulation manager against the exercise while the IT guru and a rogue metadata librarian go it alone. Wargaming has to be a shared program – even if only a few in the library, or just one, actually carry the exercises out, everyone should know what is happening and why. A couple of reasons for this.

First, a practical reason: if a record is being experimentally pranked on an out-of-date reference book (say, the Dungeons & Dragons *Monstrous Compendium* of 1989, or maybe an old telephone directory), the staff need to know about it so that anomalies are understood and more easily handled in the ILS. The circulation staff can only handle weird records if they are fully in the know about the nature and scope of the wargaming; in this case the non-system serial number that comes up when the book is marked as used or browsed in the ILS is quickly understood and dismissed, because the staff know that the *Monstrous Compendium* with the double-headed ogre on the cover has been flagged for the exercises: so expect anomalies.

The second reason to make sure everyone is aware of the RFID wargame is just good old-fashioned staff unity and cohesion. For reasons of organizational politics and morale, you will want everyone to feel respected, to feel valued, and to feel included – even when vigorous debates erupt or even if it breeds outright conflict. Presumably your organization will be robust enough to have created systems for handling conflict and disagreement among staff (if it is not, put this book down and go work on that right now). But the effect of excluding staff members from dialogue and debate about the wargames is much more damaging in the long term than any short-lived differences of opinion about what to do or not do with the RFID tags in the books for the exercises. People who work in libraries tend to identify themselves with aspects of the collections over time; doing some new and unexpected experiment which is not well understood and perhaps even seen as dangerous to the ILS, the books, or the integrity of library service is not (and should not be) easily accepted. Staff unity, even in the face of conflict over specific ideas and actions, is maintained by a certain level of communication. If no one feels that they are being intentionally ignored or mollycoddled, the library can *live* with any given amount of conflict. A sure way to wreck unity and cohesion is to misrepresent or simply not tell others what you are trying to do, and thereby cause an increase to their workload as they try to solve the 'problems' you have created in the name of experimentation. All this is to say, since wargaming arphids can become a flashpoint for cultural schism in your library, the more that is done to minimize this by being above-board, the better the health of the organization will be. So: do not wargame in secret. These exercises could be seen by the library administration and other staff members to be either beneficial, inconsequential, or outright sabotage – and this is mainly dependent on how open you choose to be about what you are doing and why. With above caveats in mind, wargaming is important and must still be done.

Begin with a decent wifi-enabled laptop (it can even be running some version of Windows). You will have purchased an RFID reader or read-writer like Socket's Compactflash

High Frequency card or a £30 Taiwanese job from Mifare/Mayday, which you can find in sources ranging from Ebay auctions, to Craigslist, to Amazon.com. Sometimes these readers can be pretty cheap, even under £5 or so, but more usually they run into the £20–£50 mark for non-commercial or small-business oriented kits. The Socket mentioned above costs in the low hundreds.

There will be software to install, and you will be able to connect the device to your laptop via Bluetooth or a USB port. The hardware for most of these devices is simply plug-and-play, so that you can begin working with RFID tags in very little time.

An RFID reader can also be used for grabbing personal and financial account data from wallets, which is one reason this field of experimentation is usually seen as very 'black hat.' With the right hardware running on your mobile device, you can snag credit card names, holder's name, expiration dates, and account numbers at a distance. The only known protection? Lining your purses and pocketbooks with something that can bounce away the radio waves, like stainless steel or aluminum foil. A cheap but effective counter-hack.

'The accessibilty of devices that can read the data, and the clustering of different kinds of data – those two factors combine to make people vulnerable' (Jardin, 2008). How you apply these lessons in your stacks is an important matter that will have wide effects in your communities. Using a variety of different kinds of information about people, from book choices to credit card numbers to the brand of shoes they are wearing, is an awful lot of knowledge and power to concentrate in one place – but the library will soon be such a place. You should start thinking about protecting your community. Wargaming identity-hack scenarios in your own stacks is a good way to begin.

A speculative near-future scenario

A patron walks up to the service desk and signs up for a replacement RFID bracelet – this century's library card. The bracelet looks like the One Campaign bracelets, but it says Read and it's striped in the colors of the village coat of arms: orange and green. Its colors match the library logo and marketing materials. It's stretchy, it's bright; it's fun to wear and cheap to replace.

As she walks through the collection browsing items, the bracelet pings those items that she picks up to read or view. The presence of the object handled, an RFID tagged book, is noted by the bracelet and its identity is recorded by serial number. She can look at thousands of items before the bracelet's memory is full. When the appropriate wand, which is just an application running through her phone, is activated near the bracelet, she can move all the serial numbers from the bracelet into her profile at the library website's bookshare application. This process can be automated so that it happens by default when she logs into an OPAC. There, she can see a graphic display of the items browsed, complete with images of covers, sample pages, citation information, blurbs and reviews, and in some cases even full text. She downloads this to her phone, leaning against an endcap in the sci-fi shelves, casting around for what she might like to read next.

Through the bookshare application, she adds names from her friends-list to the book record (*Sal oughta like this one*, she reckons, and drags his name onto a thumbnail of M. John Harrison's *Light*), automatically recommending items to those she thinks may be interested. Or she can simply keep her virtual browsing collection quiet, keeping her own notes to herself for private research. The patron decides what is shared and how. Our patron likes to share quite a lot.

Sharing agreements between multiple library systems, regional 'cards,' are also folded into the bracelet. Our patron has come some miles, walking up Keele Road from Silverdale to get access to the University Library. Wherever the patron is a member, and to whatever level the membership agreement allows access, personomic information is shared with the collection database management system of the institution that the patron visits. (If she has paid up online before her big trip, a patron from Dubai gets full digital privileges in the Library of Congress.) The bracelet is an information passport.

So she sits down in a comfy corner on the first floor of the library and settles into Iain Banks' latest, keeping a book of literary criticism on Banks nearby too. She looks up for a swig of coffee and sees a friendly face. He walks over carrying a half a dozen books stacked up in his arms.

'Ambitious, huh?' she says.

He smiles and shrugs. 'Family's going out of town. Better than watching *Flavor of Love* all weekend.'

'God, I love that show. It's a travesty. *I* would be Flav's girl.'

They chuckle. He says 'Step to me,' and asks what she's reading. They chat. Before he wanders off to the circulation desk, she asks, 'Do you mind if I ...?' and nods toward the books in his arms. He shakes his head and she waves her wrist close to his stack. She then holds her book up close to him, eyebrows arched.

'No need,' he says, 'I've already read that one. Awful ending to it ...'

He moves along.

She swigs from her bottle, and turns to the window. A biker swerves around a muscle man strolling along the sidewalk out there, and a fat robin dives from a lamp post.

Back to the real world

Much of what you may need to know about the dark nooks in the practice of identity profiling you may well learn through the workaday implementation of the increasingly popular RFID-powered self-checkout stations. Todd Humble, Supervisor at North Richland Hills Public Library near Fort Worth, Texas, is a man who knows more than most about that process.

I asked him about the most common mistakes likely to be made in implementing RFID in a collection, and he shared some tips he and his staff learned through working with many unforeseen problems that unfold in the process of RFID conversion. Here's his list, in his words (Humble, 2008):

1. Not getting an automated sorter. This piece is likely the biggest time saver of all RFID implementation products. It is typically left out due to costs but could likely save the most labor. Without the sorter there is no easy way to separate the exceptions (items returned incomplete, items with holds, etc.). It can be done with hand-held devices, but every book must be handled again.

2. Not tagging every item. Many libraries do not tag certain types of material that are problematic to tag. We have tagged 100 percent of our items so there is no need to come up with special stickers denoting that this item must be checked out at the front desk.

3. Tagging without thought as to the reader/patron who will loose information covered by the tag. Patrons dislike things being covered up that they want to read, so plan from the start not to cover certain types of information without going through the effort to scan or copy the information to make a replacement/repair piece to cover the tag.

4. Printing the barcode on the tag physically, although useful in processing this information, only presents the problem that it cannot be masked – or if it is removed there is no other identification on the item.

5. Assuming that the RFID tag replaces barcodes rather than subsidizing them. Consider that barcode tag size can be reduced and placed inside for when an RFID tag has been removed or has failed.

6. How do you property stamp your books? Consider all processes, as this conversion is the perfect time to reconsider everything and try to get it right this time.

7. Be certain to not buy a proprietary system so tag vendors may be switched as market prices drop. In less than a year we have seen another 30 percent price drop by utilizing an ISO-certified tag from a non-library-specific vendor.

8. Once you start conversion, start using the tags in circulation to ensure items will not trip gates when they are activated.

9. Realize that every RFID device likely has a different size antenna and thus a different read rate. If you convert your items before gates are installed you may be in a position that you now want to retag all your items, but at staff time premiums and tag costs this mistake could have been avoided in most cases.

10. Utilize the best quality tags available to secure your DVDs. Do not accept small hub tags unless you are guaranteed they are detectable by your gates. Utilize full-size disc tags that cover the entire disc to ensure your most desirable items are protected.

11. When creating an RFP (request for proposal) list the tags separately so you may get the best pricing on your

RFID tags. Some of the strongest tags are not currently distributed by the major library RFID vendors.

12. Don't assume shiny foil-like covers always mean that it is an RFID tag killer.

13. Test, test, and retest!

The theme from these points is plain: plan ahead carefully and test constantly. It also pulls the rug out from under one of the most common conceptions in libraries – that RFID is for the security of property. RFID can be used as a theft deterrent, but after lots of experience, Humble says flatly: 'RFID is not for theft prevention.'

I'd add one more point to the list above, just for luck:

14. Test again.

Part 3
Quality and Mettle

8

Fundamentally good service

So your library is innovative and steely-nerved. It has tried a variety of new technologies in order to get closer to the needs of its patrons, found technological solutions for information management problems, and created policies to help solve technological problems. Now it is quite clear that technology, the Webs (1.0, 2.0, 3.0 ...), social networks, and gadgets are very intimately related to the real information needs of the real people who call at your library. Technology is culture too.

This is for the public good, Mofo

Librarians have long been the guardians of culture and gatekeepers of information, or at least have imagined themselves as such. Libraries have also been the tools that the powerful use to make, break, or redefine a cultural record in terms more expedient for political ends. Alex Wright writes about the conquistadors burning the bark-covered books of the Aztecs' library, a library growing by up to 1,000 volumes a year. But this was not really the library of 'the Aztecs,' of the people. It was the library of the Aztec rulers. One hundred years before Cortes arrived, Itzcoatl 'burned the previous royal library to the ground, clearing the intellectual brush for a new Aztec history written in his own mold' (2007: 57). To this day, librarians and library administrators must fight the state in standing against censorship and co-option. Attempts to subvert us and to use us as tools in power plays will likely never cease. A long-term strategy for staying out of the governor's toolbelt is to sincerely befriend and tirelessly serve the people. By 'the people' I mean the common working public whose tax money keeps our doors open.

No amount of technological innovation in the world can replace the values that endear us to the people; technology is just another means we have to serve. This is a value statement: libraries are for the good of the people, all the people equitably, and not for the good of the powerful alone.

If it is our service that allies us to the people, then our focus as librarians must be toward pressing every advantage we have, every tool, technology, and process we have, in favor of the information needs of the people we serve. Without the people, there is no library – or there is no legitimate library. Without the library, the people have no history. This is cultural symbiosis, and it is deadly serious stuff.

Without doubt, our tools affect the nature of our services – how we serve, when we serve, where we serve, and what we serve up become modified by our technologies. I would like to think that there is a core ethos at work in libraries which might be applied universally, though the praxis issuing from this ethos will be modified locally to fit particular cultural needs as necessary.

What are the basic tenets and principles of our service? Are they the same in Magee, Mississippi as they are in Taipei, Taiwan? Are the principles similar in Mozambique and Manchester and Mumbai?

We have to think about what we exist for, what our purpose is, even if we come to different conclusions about what it is we are supposed to be doing in different parts of the world;

without mature self-reflection, we will lose our way as we try to navigate the weird paths winding out before us. We accept that we do exist (libraries do *in fact* exist), so we need not get all hung up in metaphysics. Now why do we exist? This is where that value statement above comes in: politics aside, we exist to help people access information. I am willing to up the ante and say that that is why we exist as libraries, anywhere on Earth. That is what librarianship is: we are the ones who help the people get the information. Or, said another way, we get the information to the people. And if that's not historically true, I call upon all librarians to make it true from now on.

Now from that we can derive some semi-universal points of good service which may be translated into and out of the uses of particular tools. From 'what is good virtual reference service?' or 'what is good in-person reader's advisory service?' or 'what makes a good library gaming program?' or 'how can we develop a good large-print collection?' come some essentials that can be (must be) widely applied.

We help people

You know the retarded kid that comes in with his chewed up *Pirates of the Carribean: World's End* doll, Captain Jack Sparrow's left boot just about torn off now, always asking if he can take home the latest *Game Informer* magazine? We help him. Even when he sneezes on us, we help him.

You know the old biddy with extra-crispy, blue-white hair and bright red lips, always smells like popcorn, reads lots of murder mysteries, and never smiles? You think she's a real snob. She *is* a real snob. Or she is not; but it doesn't matter. Because we help her. Even when she shoves the book down to our circulation station without a word, ignoring our *good morning ma'am*, we help her.

How about that geezer with half his teeth still waiting for him three alleys North of the library? He comes in smelling of pee, trying to sell smoke-damaged polyester neckties to the circulation staff. Normally we might help him find the door, too; but unless he's causing a disturbance, we first ask him if needs *any* help. If he needs a phone number, an address, business forms, a pencil ... And we learn what he really needs is somebody to sit down with him and teach him how to use a computer mouse. Maybe next time it'll be a job search.

We serve at the pleasure of the people. Help them as if your job depends on it. The evidence is clear: unhappy patrons will not settle for bad service – they will take their patronage elsewhere if they don't get the kind of help they need. Libraries are not the only game in town.

The Library 2.0 attitude toward serving our patrons is about much more than a top-down idea of bringing the bright ideas of the management to the checkout counter or to weekend library programs. Library 2.0 service has to be about participation with our patrons in *their* co-creation of *their* learning space. Far too often, librarians or library directors respond to suggestion box forms with glib or evasive bullet-dodging that *sounds* like the library organization is trying harder than it really is to reach out and serve. In a post-2.0 world, those comments and suggestions are referendums on management and service – and they really are not merely suggestions. They are to be taken very seriously, up to and beyond inviting patron commentators in to meet with staff and discuss solutions to issues, if the patron is willing.

The days of a degreed director skirting along on minimum and nominal service are over; the days of dismissing pleas for improvement with a sneer at the ragged and uneducated public are long, long over. If you see evidence of such days still hanging around in your library, get busy culling the attitude before you find your patrons have all abandoned you for amateur web-browsing and used book stores.

We work with information

We work with information, regardless of medium. Books are good technology – no, hold that. Books are *great* technology. They are durable, information-dense, and if the materials used in their creation are quality, they are high contrast, portable, and tolerably heat and light resistant. They don't break easily and they are very easy to share and move. Sure, we know that books are not the most efficient of all media for the transfer of information; clearly digital media is more information dense than paper (although some developments in QR Code are tilting that table). But books are good. We like books. We even like e-books and audio books recorded as mp3 files.

Libraries truck in information, in a wide variety of formats. Information exists in the form of video, as audio, as print, as hypertext, as XML schema, as realia, as ephemera, as live conversation, as performance, as smell, as Braille and other tactile interfaces. There is an infinite amount of information in the world, and it comes in an infinite variety of media and formats. Libraries should (have already) adopt(ed) Google's mission statement: to organize the world's information. Instead, we have been too particular about format and too precious about content. Often this is of necessity; after all, we cannot yet build a library of smells, or house live artists just because they have information to share in the form of performances (slinging Marmite sandwiches at a crowd, while chanting their dour hymnal selections, tearful mascara dripping on the mezzanine).

Our community's needs (the people!) must come first, and that means being mindful of and cautious with the space and resources we have been made stewards of. A responsible steward is more likely to buy and organize books than to write haiku onto the RFID tags in pigs' ears and build a slop trough in the reading room.

Conservative and responsible stewardship, however, must be balanced with openness to the infinite variety of formats. The question of format is yet another reminder that librarians have been used at times as tools of the powerful rather than of the people. Librarians have made decisions based on the political pleasure of administrators and local leaders, shelving challenged books in hard to reach spaces or requiring special access cards for graphic novel collections because a member of the elite disapproved of one of the titles of one of the people's books in the people's collection. Librarians know who feeds them, so the format and content of the information has been and continues to be format and content that please the monied or powerful so that the people's tax money will continue to flow into the library budget. We may need to find ways to rework that set-up. The variety of information in the world demands that we begin to look more honestly at our needs to expand access to new formats and into new languages, especially when the powerful find it threatening. Working with information is what we do – not just information on a Blu-ray disc or in a magazine or in a database, and not just information rubber-stamped by the bureaucrat immediately above us in the hierarchy.

Good service requires our recognition that the people we serve may need information that is not easy to get at. A student may be writing about rap syntax and beat patterns in the works of artists on the Gee Street record label from 1993 to 1998. A library has to help her get that information.

Got a listening station? Allow access to YouTube on your public Internet-access machines? She's going to need to watch some P.M. Dawn and Stereo MCs videos on YouTube or Vimeo, you know. Got music analysis software? Will you allow her to download Audacity's editor from SourceForge?

We work with information, not just books.

We teach

It's like the old Taoist proverb says: 'Give a man a fish, feed him for today; but teach a man to fish, and he's fed for a lifetime.' Libraries, no longer strictly *being* or housing collections, have to be information resources that perpetuate themselves by teaching those in our communities how to find and evaluate what they need.

We must give away the shop. It's counter-intuitive to many, but the most precious 'thing' we have (our skills, not our books), must be given away freely, thoroughly, and as quickly as possible to the communities we serve. Teaching how to do what we do well is paramount to relevance in and survival throughout the coming century.

But teaching and learning is not easy. Robert Anton Wilson (2007) said 'Nothing of any importance can be taught. It can only be learned, and with blood and sweat.' It is beyond the scope of this book to get into debates on pedagogy and teaching praxis, but as we develop and grow into our roles as teachers, we librarians would do well to remember that keeping patrons interested in database search syntax, or in points of critical thinking and information quality evaluation, will be a very serious challenge. Keeping your cool (and a positive attitude) in the face of forty unenthused students is not easy. This pain and struggle should urge us on to find better techniques and better exercises for sharing our skills. Your students will have a wide variety of learning styles and you must engage them as broadly as possible – the tactile learner, the auditory learner, the visual learner, they must all be reached, and, hopefully, they can all reach out to each other in non-traditional (that is non-lecture-based) library activities.

One important role that libraries can play is as the teachers of local history. Even as we struggle with the cultural significance of the myth that the world's collections will get systematically (even universally) scanned, digitized, indexed, and page-ranked, an unknown amount of our most important data – local data – is sitting in cardboard boxes and acidic paper bindings in the moldy closets of county courthouses and local genealogy societies. Librarians can bring this information forward by partnering with local groups. Who else is going to do this, after all? Libraries can share what they discover with schools, colleges, and governments. We can digitize and archive these riches for our local partners, and in the process become a major node of the most important history – the history of where we live. Historical societies, political organizations, and cooperatives of all kinds can join in and participate in library workshops as we all learn and teach together the forgotten stories of our own home towns.

Teaching about the communities that we serve may surprise and enlighten our patrons, but above all it will honor them. They will not soon forget it, as our connections to our places grow deeper with library-powered research, evaluation, organization, and protection of these most tender information resources.

Conclusion: no more walls

As Web 3.0 begins to have a real impact on the role of librarians as information managers, we should pause a moment to think generally about what Web 2.0 has meant and will yet mean for library service.

It is clear that Web 2.0 and Library 2.0 have made bold moves to help people to connect to other people through the power of the Internet. Web 2.0's myriad social networks and new Web utilities for linking people to people and information has underlined the need for semantic discretion and specificity within and between groups. Networks of construction contractors may refer to the term 'square' as a tool or as a state of walls and foundations; networks of Elvis fans may use the term 'square' to refer to nerds. Here we have three different concepts, different terms, represented by the sequential characters s, q, u, a, r, e. The proliferation of work groups, social groups, communities of interest, and other types of networks has created an environment in which the solutions to such semantic problems are needed more desperately than ever before.

We also live in a pro-search world, where patrons pre-emptively try to meet their own information needs without recourse to library counsel – and why not? The tools exist for our patrons to search our catalogs, or the whole world's catalogs, at a distance. As of mid-2008, Google Books alone had partnered with 19 major university and public library systems in the Americas and Europe. This collective digitization represents many millions of books which patrons can now access remotely. Our importance as guides in such an info-swamp is already recognized, but our importance as actors in a semantic network is not yet realized.

It is not the programmers, coders, engineers, and IT administrators alone who will shape Web 3.0, a burgeoning and perhaps even semi-intelligent web of natural language query, discrete and contextual meaning, and expert systems that finally rise above their humble call-and-response origins. Librarians, perhaps even while, as Bruce Sterling suggests, their skill sets are appropriated by other professions (see Appendix 1), are well positioned to build and to serve in Library 3.0. We must move quickly, however, and very earnestly, into fields many of us may find unfamiliar.

Imagine a world in which search works so well, so seamlessly, and is so pervasive, that an information seeker can ask a question of her phone or of her web browser and get an intelligent and relevant response. Why would she seek the aid of librarians? What could librarians offer her in such a world? Programs, events, gatherings, fun stuff still, surely. Librarians can pimp their bricks-and-mortar play places and get some traction out of that for a long time to come. People will gather.

And maybe librarians will be remembered in last-ditch emergencies. The semantic web is down, your patron is late for a meeting in which he has a shot at selling $2 million worth of foamboard insulation, and he needs to run some background searches on the R rating of new varieties of styrofoam. You know, there may be cases where folks still think to call us in a pinch.

But besides providing the gathering spots for story times, bitch-n-stitch sessions, and gaming marathons, and the occasional emergency 'please God help me, the Web is down' call, what will librarians do? What will libraries be? That future is up to us to write, together as professionals and with our patrons. Here are a few suggestions.

Take Library 1.0 to the Global South

It's easy to generalize and toss out glib lines about 'the third world,' but even at the risk of doing so, I think it's an area we as libraries must address our selves and our skills to. Libraries can take access to information collections and the skills to use these collections well to the impoverished of the world. Starting in your own borough, shire, parish, county, and city, figure out who lacks access and why. You may need to reach out with basic literacy classes, then expand to financial literacy, citizenship tutorials, and more advanced information literacy programs to reach the poor. Imagine a library program that offers a hot meal to anyone off the street, and has a nutritionist, a librarian, and a former rough sleeper paired up to deliver practical tips about getting the best nourishment from dumpster diving. And the librarian uses the rough-sleeping theme as content to teach basic web literacy. Poverty stricken families have information needs too – knowledge of reading, using e-mail, starting a checking account, and searching websites for jobs or grants can go a long way toward ensuring future meals and housing. Libraries have an important part to play in this, the informational aspects of people's lives.

Soon enough, once your library is earnestly serving the information needs of the local homeless, you may find ways to reach even farther afield.

Think about how our broken, damaged, and out-of-date books can be best sent to those who need them and can still get good use from them. Think about how we can use translation software to make webliographies available to folks who don't read English (there are many mediocre but free translation tools available online, like Yahoo!'s *née* Altavista's Babel Fish and Google Translator). We can use the tools we already have, with little more investment than that of time, to push services way out beyond our door, our cities, or our countries; and many libraries have been doing this, purposefully or not, since establishing web presences fifteen years ago. We can make our web presences work harder to serve those whose time on the web costs so dearly – like the kid in Buchanan, Liberia, who has saved all month to spend fifteen minutes in an Internet cafe to try and find immigration forms for Canada.

Then we can take it further.

Not many of the international aid organizations are able to move resources in the direction of information access or information literacy. There is far too much hunger, disease, and warfare that needs more urgent attention, so the focus has to be on the more immediate needs. Natural disasters affecting millions require shelter solutions, clean water, food – not libraries, not books, not laptops. Taking a longer view, however, information literacy for the world's most vulnerable people – its poor and hungry and disenfranchised – could lead to more stability, resilience, and a stronger position from which to respond to disaster, drought, and disease. Organizations like Librarians Without Borders are newly trying to make this case, and invest time and resources into the longer-term welfare of those in the developing world by bringing information access.

Other organizations are beginning to see the use of such a strategy. The networked collaboration for responding to disasters with sustainable technology and infrastructure, STAR-TIDES (Sustainable Technologies, Accelerated Research – Transportable Infrastructures for Development and Emergency Support), though mainly focusing on water filtration, solar cookers, and durable sheltering solutions, also acknowledges the role of information access in the lives of those affected by disaster. On their website (star-tides.org), ICT, or information, communication, and technology, is one of the active categories of innovation and solutions-sharing.

Communication with other family members in the area, and in other countries is a major reason to have Internet or phone access of some kind available in refugee camps; but the ability to find useful information can in itself lead to better survival and health outcomes post-disaster. Indeed, one of the most fundamental principles of STAR-TIDES is that the victims of disaster can be best helped by the availability of information and instruction from which they may learn (and modify) techniques to help them cope with extreme conditions. Efforts such as this give the management of information a place of primacy, which leads to better use and management of materials and technology to save lives and rebuild communities. Information management is something that libraries typically do very well, so it's a logical area for librarians to begin working in. (Disclaimer: I volunteer time to help with information management issues for STAR-TIDES.)

Post Web 2.0, when libraries are staring down the barrel at a semantic web 3.0 that finally kills the reference desk (see the interview with Ramona Holmes in Appendix 1), librarians can stop their shoe gazing and figure out how to contribute to these efforts. This will not just be for the good of the Global South – although any hypothetical post-junta beneficiaries of the One Laptop per Child efforts in the Irrawaddy Delta will certainly be happy, in retrospect, that somebody took the time to reach out and give them the tools that will let them build better tools and infrastructure – but we will be very well placed as central nodes in our own communities to respond to disasters and coordinate information readiness efforts and information sharing for relief workers. When Clovis, New Mexico is ravaged by tornadoes, a ready public library might be able to do plenty to lessen the suffering in Curry County by making sure the people are connected to information sources that can help them secure food, aid, and shelter.

This pre-positioning and active stance, both locally and abroad, will also work to serve librarianship itself. If a technologically leap-frogging 'third world' is already seeded with satellite versions of Libraries 1.0 through 2.0, then libraries will have a much clearer future for another fifty to a hundred years, even as libraries (as we know them) sublimate in the postmodern West, vaporized by natural language semantic search engines.

Take Library 2.0 seriously

Work through the administrative and procedural impediments to establishing profiles on social networking sites and social Web utilities. Making a mark within your network of 'friends,' your patrons, within the territory of the social software that they use daily can be a very strong statement about your library's willingness to help them wherever they may be, even when your patrons choose to spend time in territories unfamiliar to you (if, that is, the effort doesn't come across as cloying and desperate). But it is also important that we make a mark on social networking itself. Libraries have just sat back and watched as Bebo, Friendster, Hi5, MySpace, Facebook, Ning, Pownce, LinkedIn – and even corporate collaborative spaces like Microsoft's Sharepoint – have infused and influenced the activities of the daily lives of our patrons. And libraries have barely moved a toe, in comparison. Can librarians not imagine a social software suite that lets readers advise other readers of good reads? Oh wait, Amazon already did that. And so has Library Thing, Good Reads, and Shelfari. While we watch and wait for others to innovate, we become more and more doddering, seen to be more and more out of step with the needs of our community.

There is hope. Though it might be coming late to all this, OCLC's Worldcat.org could be game-changing. The OCLC (Online Computer Library Center, Inc., in Dublin, Ohio) deployed Worldcat.org in 2006. This site allows institutions (libraries mainly, of course) and individuals (anybody who wants to participate) to share information about books, websites, and even social network site profiles with other Worldcat users, to bookmark item records in any number of social utilities (from Digg to Del.icio.us, and many others), to rate items, review items, share items, tag items, and create thematic lists as subject guides for other users. What's more, users can see which libraries have access to the item. The default view for the list of libraries is geographical – the closest to your stated home locale gets the top spot on the list. Worldcat is moving in the right direction (even if they do link items' images to the Amazon store).

The web presence, and especially the catalog, of the Ann Arbor District Library (AADL – public library in Michigan, United States) is a testament to working from a Web 2.0 palette, and taking a variety of Library 2.0 initiatives to patrons online and in real life. The library's mission statement is community and activity oriented, speaking of cooperative ownership and using the library as a collective third space:

> The existence of the Ann Arbor District Library assures public ownership of print collections, digital resources, and gathering spaces for the citizens of the library district. We are committed to sustaining the value of public library services for the greater Ann Arbor community through the use of traditional and innovative technologies. (AADL, 2008)

Its catalog integrates many aspects of 2.0, including patron reviews, patron ratings of library holdings, comments, and tagging. They blog, they vlog, and they are not merely jazzing a Library 1.0 skeleton with 2.0 glitz: read about (or better yet, go participate in) their events and services and it is quite plain to see they take the ethos of response and collaboration into their daily face-to-face activities as well. They take Library 2.0 seriously.

It's the metadata, stoopid

Web 3.0 works because of metadata – data about data, information about information. Describing resources in such a way that each can be queried well in natural language is the name of the game, and more (well-formed) information is better than less.

Metadata quality, metadata automation, and creating new metadata for resources will be a major way to leverage library holdings in the next ten years. If you doubt the importance of this stream for innovation and relevance, you can browse the public budgets of technical services operations for libraries to get a sense of how valuable metadata specialists are becoming.

Many librarians recoil at the idea that they should have to become 'programmers'; we are now past the place where information managers and techies can usefully divide themselves into two separate camps. Librarians still find it useful daily to know something about book repair and book binding; today librarians also find it useful to daily add or tweak a section of JavaScript code in a library blog, or to reform the HTML headers on a library newsfeed. Tomorrow, librarians will find it useful to build XML schema indices, push cookies and easter eggs into phones, and build gestural interfaces for arphid management systems.

The world of XML and RDF can seem convoluted and confusing to the uninitiated, which is why so many librarians shy from stepping into it in the first place. Don't put it off just because you dread it. Even a bullet-point knowledge of metadata principles can go a long way toward improving your understanding of digital resources and bringing new value to your library.

RDF stands for 'resource description framework,' and is a way of describing discrete information items. A book, an article, a website, a blog post, a shoelace in an archive – all can be described in RDF. From the World Wide Web Consortium's primer on RDF (2004):

> The Resource Description Framework (RDF) is a language for representing information about resources in the World Wide Web. It is particularly intended for representing metadata about Web resources, such as the title, author, and modification date of a Web page, copyright and licensing information about a Web document, or the availability schedule for some shared resource. However, by generalizing the concept of a 'Web resource,' RDF can also be used to represent information about things that can be *identified* on the Web, even when they cannot be directly *retrieved* on the Web. Examples include information about items available from on-line shopping facilities (e.g., information about specifications, prices, and availability), or the description of a Web user's preferences for information delivery.

Learning to make use of RDF for web resources and shifting away from MARC for web-based book records, as Roy Tennant and others have advocated (Tennant, 2007), can do much to make our collections more findable and usable for our patrons, and for folks just hunting for information anywhere in the world.

The more particular our collections are – and this has a lot to do with how involved we choose to be with our local community clubs and organizations – the more important this findability may become. Say, for example, there is a set of architectural notes made by Fay Jones when he was getting small jobs in Mississippi, and those notes are now under the stewardship of the historical society of the town of Bay Saint Louis, on the coast of the Gulf of Mexico. The library and the historical society can work together, creating metadata and digital copies of these notes to share with the rest of the world, and thereby make an important resource for twentieth-century architecture available to all. Storms come and storms go, but we must build the information resources, partnerships, communities, and infrastructures that stay and stand and serve no matter what.

Even the use of a metadata mill, like the Dublin Core machine at Worthington Memory (*http://www.worthington memory.org/DC_Form.cfm*), can help bring a library and its partners far into good metadata practice. In fact, the Worthington Memory mill itself was created through a partnership between the Worthington Historical Society in Ohio and Worthington Libraries. This is exactly the kind of mutual growth through resource sharing that can bring rare local information into the light for researchers.

Good morning and good luck

The world is in ferment and it is a new century for librarianship. Your skills are going to take your patrons farther than you think. As the information revolution continues and the Internet continues to grow from the advent of the Web, then of Web 2.0, we now see the semantic web unfolding just ahead. Library 3.0 will be built soon on the foundations we square and level today.

Libraries are changing now and transforming patrons' lives because of what you do today. You matter more than you know.

Be brave.

Appendix 1
The interviews

Dialogue with Jessamyn West, September 2008

Jessamyn is a librarian consultant in rural Vermont, a writer and library blogger, and a moderator for the popular 'community weblog' Metafilter.com. Here we talk about copyleft, copyright, privacy, and how it all affects our patrons.

WE: Privacy, seems to me, hasn't gotten much play in the library world compared to other issues. Why is it more important now than it was, say, five years ago?

JW: Well, I think because libraries are moving more into people's 'regular lives' so to speak. So privacy used to mean 'we won't tell people what you're reading, we won't tell people where you live' and now it's got more to do with people's computer habits, laws regarding computer habits [Children's Internet Protection Act (CIPA, 2000) and Children's Online Privacy Protection Act (COPPA, 1998)] and libraries interacting with patrons in more different ways. So, for example, what does privacy mean as far as retaining log files from a web server [and who even owns those] or sign up sheets on a computer? Or IM transcripts for reference, or similar stuff ... more and more we don't even *own* the records we try to keep private, and at the same time the governmental climate, in the US anyhow, has changed and people are more fearful of people with 'something to hide' and seem to think that if you're requesting privacy you're shady. I think that's a bad trend.

At the same time we have vendors like OCLC and others basically saying that our commitment to privacy is keeping us from being able to fully engage with patrons in this 2.0 world, and I think that's flat out nonsense. But they're putting pressure on libraries to get more 'relaxed' about privacy. That rankles me.

WE: I saw a video of you at ALA after a session you did with [the science-fiction author and boingboing.net blogger] Cory Doctorow, drawing out some of the themes from his novel *Little Brother*. In the video, you mentioned the idea of a granulation of privacy. Can you unpack how libraries might go about this, and how we could sell the concept to our communities? Is it a 'sliding' level of privacy for different needs?

JW: I just think we could do a better job protecting people's privacy in real ways, not like fakey ways that can be socially engineered. If I were solving this problem with my techie hat on, I'd say something more like 'hey we can encrypt your records, that way you have access to them and we can use not personally identifiable data within them for record keeping but only you can link it to yourself ...' and then people could own their *own* data. But that means teaching people about tech, which we suck at, as libraries, mainly because we've been pushing bad tech in people for so long they don't trust us anymore with regards to technology. But it's not that hard to make data really private – the hard part is: 1. figuring out if patrons are willing to take some of the responsibility for their data remaining private [see Sarah Palin's e-mail hacked, oy!] and 2. getting staff to think that's a good idea.

I think we talk the talk about privacy a lot but don't even personally walk the walk, much less at an institutional level.

So thinking about different data like web server logs, traces people leave on public computers, OPAC records, ILL records, patrons' private data, etc. All of those can be individually obscured and at the same time be used in the aggregate to deliver better services. It would be cool as an example to have a sort of 'patrons who read this also read that' feature, and vendors would love to sell it to us, but they say our commitment to privacy is what's keeping them back. And I don't buy that. At the same time I think we could build tools like this ourselves that came with strong privacy features *built in* and stop having this fight over and over. Another thing that has changed in the past decade is that people are more used to having less privacy, more security cameras, more sites asking for personal information and giving you something [access to your network] in return and so our commitment to privacy seems outdated in some ways but I see it more to the point as being needed more than ever, honestly.

WE: Also, how does the ramping up of private subcontractors doing libraries for cities and government agencies change the conversation? Could they claim ownership of patron data?

JW: Sure, anyone who trafficks the data could claim that their policies are what are the relevant policies that attach to the data. It's totally sketchy. And the more we moved to hosted solutions for things [where the data lives at a server that is somewhere other than inside our own libraries] we have to closely examine privacy policies and answer tough questions about what we do if there's a breach, etc. I mean lately, it's been crazy – credit card companies and banks are losing people's private data all the time, and at the same time as they try to sell us tools to prevent this. But our biggest risks are people breaching bank security, in my opinion.

WE: Why are citizens giving away their rights to tinker with their own info anyway? Whatever happened to 'the people's library'?

JW: Well that's a good question, right? It's never been true that the people had the keys to the building. They never had access to the library basement. And that's okay, really; you sort of hire your librarian to take care of those sorts of things for you. *But* in terms of data and data security, your librarians are not handling it. No one is handling it. And so we wind up in this sort of mess that we're in where ALA starts a big PR campaign about how we care about people's privacy. But if I had to bet, I'd bet that most librarians don't even know how to clear the web caches of their public access computers.

WE: An important theme in this book is learning how to hack our own stuff. How can we create a culture of ownership/'white hat' hackership in our library communities? In your view, would that be a step toward solution? I notice you do Ubuntu ...

JW: Good question. Again, I don't see our libraries as really set up for the distributed model of managing data or web stuff generally. I mean a big part of 2.0 stuff is user-generated content, but librarians can often get freaked out enough just by thinking about people leaving comments on their blogs that they don't move to the next step. Basically to think about patron data you have to think about where it is now: locked up in proprietary ILSes, often in non-standard data formats, and that doesn't even touch things like online database collections, where it would be easy to be able to track things, save your own data, differentiate it from others, etc.

So tools like Zotero help with that [sort of a citation tracker that works inside your browser] and they only work because open source tools like Firefox exist for communities to build around and into. So a lot of it is resource management – 'Too broke to do something? Spend less money on software licensing, for a start ...' But open source people can sometimes be smug, or a little 'my way or the highway' about things, and have to realize that we're starting from a really unsophisticated position where the Gates Foundation gave public libraries a lot of our computers and sort of dumped them in our laps and locked them down and made us feel that our patrons, even touching the computers, were a threat to them – which really meant that IE was an insecure browser and Win2K was an insecure operating system, but this was foisted on a lot of librarians who didn't know tech very well and just sort of trusted the authorities in this case.

So I guess my list of things is:

1. Librarians need to take more responsibility for being savvy tech consumers.

2. Libraries as institutions need to decide what their values are with regard to resources that are becoming increasingly (a) digital and (b) rent-to-own situations.

3. Other options need to be considered realistically if the current ones aren't working.

4. More cooperation between institutions at a national level, in my opinion, needs to happen.

WE: What do you think about RFID in library cards?

JW: I think managed well it's not so terrible, but that it won't be managed well. That's about it really, I think RFID is a red herring.

WE: RFID seems fertile for privacy abuse. Microsoft and others, you know, have plans to make commercially available personal RFIDs for grocery stores, etc. I just want a way to opt out, or like you talk about above, at least give our patrons a way to buy in and have some control if libraries do begin using such systems.

JW: Yeah totally – and I don't see that happening which bums me out. It feels weird to say, but I don't hate RFID, I just dislike proprietary implementations where we have no idea what's going on, like at the supermarket. I literally do not care if people know what I eat and when I was there, etc. But I know other people do, and I don't like being looked at as some sort of criminal when I don't want to give people my driver's license to get a supermarket discount card. I think it's coercive, really, and just like we should be proactive about telling people they can opt out of our stupid filters we should do the same for RFID unless we can *guarantee* their data is safe – because that's what privacy really is. If someone can wave an RFID wand near me and get my credit card information off my wallet, then someone is not keeping my information safe. Librarians should be able to answer those questions from their patrons, and be firm with their vendors about the same thing. We won't have control if libraries decide to use this stuff, I think. That's sort of a problem: it's something you can't take back, possibly. And it's weird because generally speaking I'm in favor of letting the librarians make the decisions about how to run the library and I bristle when techie people are like 'my library is so stupid, they do this stupid thing and have this dumb system why won't they let me do the work *for free*, they are so stupid.' But really I get how the system works and how real change is slow, and that's okay for venerable institutions of knowledge and storage – not so much for tech-savvy info commons places.

WE: In terms of Web 2.0 and its future molting into Web 3.0, do you have any words of caution or advice for librarians looking to help build Library 2.0?

JW: Well, one of the things I tell people all the time is that none of the 2.0 stuff means giving up the things we already do, but we need to talk about privacy differently and differentiate what's patron data that we sort of control [OPAC stuff, address/phone stuff] and what's stuff we don't control [Facebook data, MySpace data, webmail data] and be ready to answer patron questions. But just because we're reachable in Facebook doesn't mean that we in any way are responsible for Facebook's privacy policy (nor should we be), but the 2.0 world is making us have to evaluate just how much we care about privacy in terms of reaching beyond traditional notions like 'we won't tell people what book you're reading' and some people seem to be up to the challenge of thinking about all this in these new ways. I think a lot more of us are going to have to really evaluate our policies, about privacy, about Internet access, about filtering, about interacting with patrons generally, and that's just going to be part of being a librarian in 2008 and beyond, so we need to be ready for that.

WE: Seems to me libraries are well past due for a frank discussion with their communities about 'digital rights management' software. Patrons bring in media and software to use on our machines, and we may end up with the raw end.

JW: It's not even talking to their communities, I think they have to talk to themselves about it as well. We know that the licensing and laws with regard to digital media are different than with books. There is no right of first sale with digital media. So when you buy a DVD, for an easy example, you don't quite own it like you do with a book. This gets even more complicated with stuff like audiobooks through Overdrive, an example I use often, which has 'checkoutability' thanks to intrusive DRM. But the checkoutability comes at a cost, and that cost is that the media is hard to use, has onerous licensing and becomes something we pay for over and over and over again [yearly in this case unless I am mistaken], and we have to explain to patrons why this audiobook can't be downloaded to a Mac and can't be put on the most popular mp3 player *of all time*. So they look at us like we're idiots in some ways, and I can't blame them. It's epic on the confusing scale. It's like health care in the US – the reason it's so confusing is that certain people want to protect their financial interests. There is *nothing* about the technology inherently that makes it hard, at *all*. But for us, trying to give away digital media for free – like we did with books – its being hampered, directly, by licensing companies who want to be able to tell us what we can and can't do with the things we purchase. DVD companies even tell us how we can or can't advertise a showing of a particular movie! It's totally insane, and we act like the RIAA [Recording Industry Association of America] is like the police, that they've been granted their powers by the state – which is sort of true and sort of not true. But I'd personally like to see some good old-fashioned civil disobedience surrounding this issue. Is the MPAA [Motion Picture Association of America] really going to come after a public library who showed a four-year-old Harry Potter movie because they used the name of the movie in their town of 5,000 people? Really? I bet no. And it's obnoxious to think that's an appropriate way to spend anyone's money or time.

So yes, I totally agree – but to explain this problem or make policy about it, you must first understand it. And libraries are so used to getting information from 'the experts' that we're in a complicated position where the same people who are the 'experts' are also the people with the vested interests in keeping our money and locking up our content, including our own government embarrassingly enough. (Ashcroft and beyond attorney generals talking about how copying a movie is theft, shame on them!) So that's my major angle, I feel like I'm helping by talking straight about it, and explaining stuff to people, but I really feel like the profession views me as a crank in some ways just for feeling that way and talking about it.

And that sort of annoys me a little.

WE: I don't think you're a crank. Speak truth to power!

JW: Hee, there's not a lot of activists in the library world. And a lot of the ones that are there are cranky anti-tech people who I don't get along with.

WE: Well, what are you up to now, and through 2009? Any major new actions we should know about?

JW: Not really. I'm trying to do more public speaking and a little less unpaid work, even though it's tough because there are a lot of things I'd love to do equally. Now that working for MetaFilter is a paid job and I have my own apartment (I was a house-sitter for a few years), I feel like I have more stability to really manage more stuff ... So, other than 'more!' nothing special.

WE: Thanks for your time. It's great to get your perspective. Keep fighting!

Dialogue with Ramona Holmes, January 2009

Ramona is a metadata librarian who leads the Information Organization Department for the University of Texas at Arlington (Arlington, Texas). She has worked in public and academic libraries in a wide variety of roles, and is now working hard to make sure libraries remain relevant and useful to new generations of students and scholars. Here we talk about the semantic web, and how it may impact librarians.

WE: The 'semantic web' is coming, and clearly metadata is key. How can libraries position themselves to be relevant in metadata management and the Web that comes next?

RH: To remain relevant catalogers must be open-minded about our long-standing standards (AACR2 and MARC) being outdated. However, we are trapped with millions of these records. So the question is how can we take those records and make them available via the semantic web? Obviously, XML can be used to 'translate' the MARC records into something more relevant, but this only takes care of today. Metadata professionals (formerly known as catalogers) have to think beyond our standards and accept that things are not perfect. FRBR/RDA will have a huge impact on how we create cataloging records. For example, take a look at your local OPAC and then take a look at fictionfinder.oclc.org (*http://fictionfinder.oclc.org*), OCLC's prototype using FRBR. It looks very much like Amazon. Libraries must be willing to take risks and accept that failure is the essence of evolution. :)

WE: How did you get interested in this stuff?

RH: I have been in libraries for half my life. I am institutionalized at this point. :) Cataloging is like a quest, you have to find the exact place to put this object or it makes it hard for others to complete their quests. However, the playing field is no longer the stacks where you work, it's the Web – and there is no perfect place to put one object. So I had to think about all the ways people find things, rather than one elusive, perfect spot which is how I was taught to catalog. The complexity of a global knowledge base is much, much more interesting.

WE: It seems like this field within library science is edging into computer science turf. What is your attitude toward service and outreach strategy? We should be able to market ourselves and our services better than the IT folks and gearheads, right?

RH: These sciences are blending; I see it in the programs offered by library schools. For example, what was 'The Library and Information Science School' at the University of North Texas is now called 'The College of Information, Library Science and Technologies' and pulls from telecommunication, computer science, information science, and education fields. I think this is amazing progress. For example, I have two colleagues from UNT, all of us took an almost identical set of courses which leaned toward the technology aspect of our field. Of the three of us, I am the only one actually working in libraries, managing a metadata unit. One colleague runs the servers for EDS, and the second is a web designer for Travelocity. It is good that information science trained individuals are infiltrating other fields. They bring with them a core commitment to service that is found in most library schools and, frankly, the corporate world needs this kind of mentality. To market yourself as an information professional is definitely twenty-first-century librarianship.

WE: What's at stake if librarians screw this up?

RH: We will become obsolete. Who needs us when any ol' information becomes acceptable? Librarians must remain relevant by inserting our expertise in the technology of Web 2.0 and the semantic web. For example, spend time populating the AADL.org folksonomy with terms that make sense to 'civilians' not just librarians. Spend an afternoon adding some of your personal library to LibraryThing so that other people can use a trained professional's expertise by pulling from your collection. These are the things we should be doing.

WE: Are there, say, four or five 'top mistakes' librarians are making in terms of preparing for the semantic web?

RH: Don't ignore change simply because you think librarians already do it better. It is critical to find ways to make ourselves relevant in terms of Web 2.0 technologies and this does not mean just learning about them.

Not being technical minded; this is more than just using a database to find things. Understand how the database is constructed and you will be able to find things better. This actually happens now with our current standards. I get questions from reference staff that if they simply understood MARC, and how it indexes, they would have been able to resolve the issue.

Challenge our stereotypical image as guardians of the books and 'expert shushers.' Libraries should be centers of the community – be it a city, campus, etc. This has been happening for a decade so it's not really all that new, except I still find quiet libraries which creep me out.

WE: How soon till you obviate reference librarians?

RH: I make this statement all the time, mostly to irritate reference librarians: 'Each time a customer locates information, without using reference, I have done my job. Therefore, if metadata personnel do our jobs well, then why will people need reference?' It's easy to spot the trend that people would prefer to 'Google it' than ask someone else, not that this is the best idea in all cases. However, with places like Wikipedia being used as sources for information, where does reference fit it? Also, looking at Amazon, in a public library why would you ask a librarian, 'What's a good book' when you can check Amazon for reviews and 'if you like this ... try this' from peers instead of librarians? This goes back to the semantic web question and probably my whole point, if it's described well and in language that makes sense (non-librarian jargon), will people actively seek reference to answer questions or simply make decisions based on what they find that is convenient?

Dialogue with Bruce Sterling, June 2008

Bruce Sterling, the science-fiction writer who helped to define the cyberpunk genre, has since written widely about design and ubiquitous computation – see especially *Shaping Things* (2005). I asked him about search, spimes, and libraries.

WE: Libraries fret lots about becoming irrelevant, and plenty of us librarians try to stress that it's our skills rather than our collections that will be key to our survival. What do you reckon, are libraries or librarians going to be around in another hundred years?

BS: They'll be around if people use them. Otherwise they're heading for the elephant's graveyard of dead media, rather like the formerly giant collections of leather Latin scrolls.

There are more than a few librarian 'skills,' but they might get unbundled and appropriated by other professions.

WE: It irritates the hell out of us when folks say 'Google it', because we see search engines as great tools – a great hammer. But you've got to know how to use the hammer or you will end up with a bad, um, building. How do you think librarians can best go about teaching proper hammer-use?

BS: Search engines are very fluid and developing rapidly, so I wouldn't categorize them as hammers. I would point out that they beat the hell out of all other forms of research in speed and convenience, so skeptics run the risk of coming across like cranks who don't trust paper money and insist on trading with solid, high-quality gold.

I'd suggest some kind of 'best-practices' bureau where librarians can teach other librarians about 'good' uses of 'bad' search engines.

WE: You've got one foot in Europe. Is the kind of skepticism toward American-born digitization projects as expressed by Jean-Noel Jeanneney common in writers and designers there, or is this just French anglophobia?

BS: It's just French anglophobia. Europeans are keenly aware that the Web came out of CERN, so you don't see all that many skeptical attacks on, say, the semantic web of Sir Tim Berners-Lee.

Also there have been attempts to build a French-centric search engine and much French struggle to 'reform' the 'dark-age' Internet to make it more friendly and profitable for the French culture industry. The French got as much right to try this as anybody else, and if they end up as the only polity where novelists get paid to do anything, I might end up moving to France.

WE: What areas can librarians and technologists work for real 'viridian' changes? Information management is core to your ideas on spimes, but have you identified particular tactical points for implementing sustainable design? If so, how do librarians help?

BS: Well, I've lectured and published rather extensively on the futuristic topic of 'ubiquitous computing in the service of sustainability.' It's a grand theoretical topic, but if it becomes a reality, I'm pretty sure it will start in small hotspots of practice where the many kinks can be worked out, and then it will spread. I would suggest that librarians interested in sustainability might want to consider what librarian skills could offer for physical objects: in manufacturing processes, in distribution, in retail, and especially in creating, building and maintaining archives of the use of objects. I've suggested that 'information architects' would be the proper profession for an effort like this, but maybe 'library science' would have more to offer.

That sounds kind of forbidding and complicated, so let me put it this way. Imagine you had a private 'library' of everything you had ever bought, used or owned. How could you use that resource to teach yourself to live better?

WE: Your view of search engines as fluid and quickly developing only reminds me of the deficiencies of search. There hasn't been any thing truly conceptually new in search since 1998. We have no video, image, or audio able algorithms that don't depend on text transcripts, keywords, or subject descriptors. Were you referring to moves toward the semantic web, Web 3.0? I recently had an ex-Assistant Secretary of Defense remind me that 'we need to automate the collection of metadata for disaster relief efforts'; well, despite Web 3.0 hype, none of this can be automated yet. Metadata (and meaning) must still be hand plucked and preened by human agents. How seriously do you regard the semantic web?

BS: As a writer, I naturally love the idea of a semantic web. Still, a real, true, deep semantic web ought to manipulate language and meaning more effectively than humans can; so it ought to be able to pass a Turing Test, which I don't consider plausible.

I don't doubt that librarians find search deficient. Google Translator is also rather deficient. Still, the thing more or less translates without human aid and the pragmatic effects are astonishing. There hasn't been anything 'conceptually new' in machine translation in ages, either, but if there are huge statistical piles of data combined with brute-force server farms, then from a user's perspective, it's a big deal. You've got a search engine that will search in multiple languages and present the results in the (mangled) language you choose. Find me a library that does that.

Then there's Google Maps. Nothing particularly new there either, except that it's fast and it works and everybody uses it. An objection to a fait accompli of that kind is best described as 'academic.'

WE: That private library of 'everything you've ever bought, used, or owned' you mentioned – how do we use this not as a personal tool, but as a community (not communal) tool for learning how to live better and use our resources (including information) better in plurals?

BS: I don't doubt that there are groups and organizations who would find a spime-like technology useful. Likely those would be places and situations with tight physical constraints and a high premium on knowing the location and identity of resources. So: prisons and concentration camps; emergency shelters; hospital emergency rooms; military camps; ships; offshore platforms; clean-rooms and assembly facilities; shipping warehouses – basically, any place that's already benefiting from 'real-time locating systems.' By mentioning concentration camps I want to make it clear that this is not a value-free technology.

Adam Greenfield seems to think that the natural laboratory of 'everyware' is cities. Urbanware, urban informatics, and that the platform of choice is the cellphone. He may be right. So maybe the proper 'community' is an entity like Tokyo or New York. Imagine yourself as a librarian-information architect-urban explorer.

It sounds like an exciting career.

Dialogue with Lori Bell, Summer, 2008

Lori Bell is one of the founders of Second Life Library and Director of Innovation at The Alliance Library System. She is very patient with me. I blogged negatively (well, skeptically) about Second Life at ISHUSH (www.ishush.blogspot.com) more than once, but she still agreed to be an interview subject for my book. Here we talk about why librarians ought to give virtual worlds a chance.

WE: Lori, I am skeptical of Second Life as a means to 'get the information to the people.' The Second Life Library (or libraries?) itself usually just directs patrons to URLs on the Web outside of Second Life. Are there any means unique to Second Life for conveying information?

LB: There are means unique to Second Life to convey information – to create an information experience. The reference desk on Info International is staffed about 80 hours per week by volunteer librarians and library staff from all over the world. As in regular libraries, many of the questions are directional or unique to the community – Second Life. Other questions might be to connect an educator or librarian with someone in Second Life with the information or expertise needed. Libraries are also promoting books through immersive environments and numerous book discussions. Immersive environments are ways in which libraries can convey information not available in real life. For instance, we have Renaissance Island, an environment in Tudor Times when Elizabeth was Queen. There is a reproduction of the Globe Theater where instructors and students can practice a play, learn about theater and Shakespeare. The homes are built with historical accuracy and students, instructors, and Second Life residents can rent and furnish a home. There are shops, a church, a manor house, and many other builds. Residents and visitors can role-play, simply participate or observe. Some role-play areas in Second Life are very strict about dressing in the time period and the mannerisms of the period. On Renaissance, one can do what one is comfortable with. There is a library in the manor house with links to web resources, information on books and other resources about the period, etc. Many of the items on the island can provide more information about themselves with a click on the item and a notecard of information. Another example of this as a way to share information is Land of Lincoln which has a period era White House, a plantation with resources about slavery, a Lincoln Memorial, a recreation of Lincoln's home in Springfield, and a nineteenth-century village. On Renaissance and on Lincoln, another way to share information is through immersive events with jousting, music and dancing of the period, historical re-enactments by avatars of Henry VIII, Abraham Lincoln, Mary Lincoln, and others.

WE: Why did Alliance Library System decide to get into this?

LB: Alliance Library System got involved when in April 2006 I read an article in *Business Week* about real people making their real life living in Second Life. There was not an active library so we decided to build a small experimental library to see if people would use it. We did not anticipate the number of librarians and library staff from all over the world who decided to get involved, volunteer, and share their time and expertise. The project grew very quickly and is now not so much Alliance as the people involved. There are core library services which include collections, reference, etc. offered in the regular library. There are also collaborative efforts where librarians set up a presence for their library or university and then work with other librarians and educators to share expertise.

WE: Where does Alliance see this going?

LB: Alliance and the librarians in the project see this as another place libraries may want to consider offering services, as they do in their physical library, as they do on their websites. Gartner Research Group predicts that by 2011, 80 percent of Internet users will be in virtual worlds. Many people see this as the next evolution of the Internet, of the Web, and we would like to see libraries in a leadership proactive role instead of reactionary after things are already developed. Many of the librarians who work in corporations which are in Second Life have major roles in the training of employees and development of virtual world presences (Sun, IBM, etc.).

WE: Does Second Life Library have any interesting partners in Second Life (or real life)? What kinds of projects can come out of partnering with a virtual institution like the Library?

LB: The Second Life Library has a number of great partnerships and collaborations that we might not have in real life. In March we planned a virtual world's education, libraries, and museums conference. The New Media Consortium (NMC) worked with us and provided a conference site for us. We partnered with staff from IBM and Sun who worked on the conference with us. Libraries of all types are involved in Second Life and partner with one another to provide services and programs. We also have people from other educational disciplines involved in our library groups. We have been able to partner with Learning Times, a leader of online conferences in offering the Stepping Into History (*http://www.steppingintohistory.org*)

conference which has been very successful. These conferences are revenue generators which will pay for the library presences in Second Life.

WE: The idea that the 'unique means' to convey info in Second Life is the immersive models itself/themselves is really interesting. But after spending time exploring the recommended models for education (like the NOAA island's hurricane, etc.), it seems that the strength of Second Life is not its ability to model things well, because the models are still clunky and inexact. Rather, it seems to me, the strength of this immersion must be the skills required to build and access the models. Is that, the building and finding skill set, something libraries ought to focus on teaching?

LB: You are right – parts of Second Life are still clunky. However, Second Life is the best of what is out there right now as far as virtual worlds go. There are dozens of worlds and each offers something different. Right now, although Second Life is clunky, the others are clunkier. Things are changing and developing so quickly I don't think virtual worlds will be clunky for long. The strength of the immersion is the skills to build the models and design the experience. I think libraries should act as knowledge guides and connect people. They may or may not be knowledgeable about how to build, but they will know who to ask or where to go to find the information for the person. They can also help builders and developers to create interactive experiences and provide the interactive information to make the experience better.

WE: How should libraries handle real-life animosity toward Second Life when testy city council members think the library is wasting resources and denying real-life service?

LB: I think libraries should have factual information about how many people are using and will use virtual worlds in the future, have experts on hand to come and talk to them about positive results for their library, be up front about the problems and challenges and how they will be handled, and share collaborative efforts that show the library is not denying real-life services. For example, we are working on collaborative reference services so that if a library contributes two hours per week at a collaborative desk then their patrons have access to the services 24/7.

WE: Do you see any ways for real-life groups, say a group that has formed around Meetup.com, to use Second Life to enhance (not replace!) real-life interactions? If that were possible, it seems there would be lots of opportunities for hybrid library programs.

LB: What great possibilities. One way these could be enhanced is if there is not an interest group in the person's own geographic area, maybe the group could have some meetings in a virtual environment so people could join no matter where they are geographically. I predict there will be more and more hybrid programs – a combination of in-person and online, in-person and Second Life, etc.

Appendix 2
Tips, tricks, and hacks:
some ideas

What follows is a list of ideas. I have either tried these myself, seen them implemented by others, or have heard the suggestion from colleagues. The quality of the outcomes of these ideas depends on the context in which they are tried, how hard you are able to work on them, and what kind of organizational environment supports you. Since most of these are about reaching out to and working with your community, the success of these ideas will also hinge on your library's ability to stoke the passion of its patrons. These are just ideas, but some have seen winters; they come out of fifteen years' experience in all kinds of library settings, from warfighting, to tea parties. Try them at your own risk.

Build a library of documents online

It is possible to build a small online library for the core documents of a historical society, a church or coven, a writer's workshop, or most any other project for no cost except that of a librarian's time. Using Google webspace (Google Pages) to build the site, and using a Google Custom Search Engine, you can soon create a small would-be web-based OPAC. You may prefer to do this with space on your own servers, and with or without the search power of Google: you can modify this plan in any way you see fit.

Metadata is important in any library, but becomes especially important when there is no MARC record for the documents. Compose a template in text or HTML for pulling the metadata elements on each of the documents in your library. You will have many choices for which metadata standard to employ. Beginning with a Dublin Core generator (like the one mentioned above at Worthington Memory) to maintain consistency is a good idea, particularly since Dublin Core is so widely used. Over time, it may become apparent that your documents would be more useful to your own *communities of interest* if they were in some other standard. But Dublin Core is still a good beginning, because other standards tend to be either based upon or closely related to it. For example, the DDMS (Department of Defense Metadata Specification) format, though it includes specifications particular to military logistics, is based on Dublin Core (and DDMS is related to the standards used by disaster relief agencies as well).

With help from knowledgeable sources inside your own patron base, you can prioritize the details of essential and non-essential elements to include in your metadata, arrange them in order of importance, and gain insight into other issues. Create a template that is both easy for you to work with, and useful to non-librarians in your community.

As members of your group make documents available for the online collection, you should be able to identify the major elements of metadata (title, author, date of composition) easily. The trickier points (format, identification, relations) must be reached through discussions with your community about the nature of the document. Your catalogers might be kind enough to lend you a hand with some of this, but there are also plenty of tutorials and explanations of metadata formats available.

In time, you will want to begin to get a sense of which elements your community needs and which they do not. It may not even be necessary to generate metadata for all element fields. In your webspace, you may create a page with the metadata as plain text or with minimal formatting (and write the metadata elements in the page code), create a title, date, and description template, for every document page, and, finally, link directly to the document on the server. A browsable list of documents is helpful, depending on the size of your library, and this might even be faceted. A search-engine powered catalog will be useful for your community too, and is likely to be preferred by most over title or date browsing.

Finally, think about usage rights and intellectual property. Do you or your organization have the right to reproduce these documents? Are permissions on file? Will you want to grant a Creative Commons license for their future use and modification, or is it better to clamp down with a strict copyright and call it done? Local laws and corporate policies may factor into these decisions.

For a sample online documents library, take a look at the STAR-TIDES document archive at *http://project.star.tides .googlepages.com/*. Other examples of similar projects are plentiful on the Web.

Establish a book-swap rack

Whether yours is a military, corporate, public, or academic library, people who come into your library like to see what other people are reading. Given a venue, people will meet to talk about books and share them. Libraries are famously good in this area (though large chain book stores are gaining ground on libraries as likable and active third places), and it's a strength we all should find new ways to play to.

One low-maintenance way to encourage such an atmosphere (even if you don't have Library Thing for Libraries, a speaker's corner, or enough room to keep up a ThinkeringSpace) is to establish a space for book swapping. This can be a shelf, a cart, or a rack. The spinning or rotation-style racks for paperbacks is a good choice for such a space. A bit of signage clearly marking the rack with some wording like 'Leave a Book, Take a Book' should be enough to start. You might stock the rack with a few paperbacks to begin – and these could even be cheap, damaged, or donated – to get patrons to stop and browse. Soon enough, patrons will bring in books and take away books, and the variety may surprise you. The rack's collection will become as diverse as the interests of your patrons.

The rack may itself become a draw to the library, bringing by folks who know that they can pop in, leave off something they weren't crazy about (or liked well enough to pass along), and pick up something new. In time, regulars may even begin leaving messages for other readers in margins, or in sticky-notes stuck onto favorite sections, marking out favorite passages .... the exchange of information doesn't have only to burgeon online.

Word2Wiki Code

If you have documents in Microsoft Word format that you need to port into an internal knowledge base running MediaWiki (this is one of the more common wiki softwares – developed by the WikiMedia Foundation, this is the same wiki markup as Wikipedia), you can use a macro to mark up the document in Microsoft Word, then copy and paste it into your wiki editor. This is great for building your knowledge base quickly, when you have many years worth of backlogged procedural or policy documents saved as Microsoft Word files.

In short order, thousands of pages can be marked up as wiki documents, copied wholesale and pasted into the wiki editor for further collaborative tinkering. The promise of the (relative, only relative) ease of such transitions from Word .doc files into wiki-ready formatting can be an incentive to help members of your team come out from locked away procedures, and share more readily with others. As team leads trying to move their organizations into wiki-based knowledge management systems know too well, anything that makes the process of transition into collaboration easier for the guarded 'old guard' is worth some consideration.

Here are the steps:

1. Copy the appropriate code at the Word2Wiki article here: *http://meta.wikimedia.org/wiki/Word_macros*.

2. Paste it into a notepad and save it as word2wiki.bas.

3. Open the MS Word document you will convert.

4. Start Visual Basic in Word (Alt + F11).

5. In VB select File → Import file.

6. Then browse to your word2wiki.bas and select it.

7. Click Run, and it converts that Word file into wiki markup, which you can copy and paste into your wiki.

This process comes from Wikimedia's Word macros page, and was put into practice and refined with the team at Appropedia.org (Chris Watkins and Curt Beckmann in particular).

Quick and dirty indexing

There will be reference books which have no online indices. These may be local or regional histories, biographical dictionaries, gazetteers, genealogies; maybe these are large, well-known, internationally common sets, but your library has chosen not to purchase a license to its online database content. Whatever the case, you can create your own electronic database of reference indices: a meta-index for your reference collection. There are a number of reasons for pursuing this project, but the time and energy involved is not negligible, so be sure to spend some time discussing this with reference staff to make sure this is a direction beneficial for your team. If you find yourself repeatedly consulting the same sources and searching the indices for similar topics often, then this may be worth the time.

To begin, identify those reference books and indices that you will need to index. Scan these indices with a digital document camera or laser scanner, creating file folders for each reference book. PDF may be the most all-round useful format for this, but you will have to determine questions of format based on your own needs. Ultimately you will end up with several folders, each perhaps containing scores of files, and each file containing one or two pages worth of index.

Create a new PDF document, in which you place all of the index files you have scanned. You may wish to organize these index sets by call number, alphabetically, or by some other system (most to least used, thematically, by class assignments if you serve an academic population, etc.), and then of course in sequence as they appeared in the original reference set. Optical character recognition software will be key to the success of this project. You will end up with a very large document (whether PDF, or in HTML, XML, or plain text format), which will be entirely searchable. A Control + F search box allows search of the entire new meta-index; or, if you like, a custom search engine can be constructed to search a series of these index pages on your server (with a tool like Google Custom Search).

- *Benefits*. At a busy reference desk, librarians can quickly find a mention of any term indexed in any reference set with one search, then go directly out to that source with the patron and find the subject in question without poring through multiple print indices. This is very useful in a large public or academic library, or in an under-staffed library. The ability to search all of your print reference resources in seconds and take your patron directly to the relevant sources is a huge step forward.

- *Challenges*. In the scanning process, it will be important to formulate a system for noting the titles and locations of the sets on every page of every index. Usually titles would be in the header or footer, along with pagination, but the call numbers will not be – it may behoove you to supply them, but this will increase the workload of the project substantially unless a way to automate the process is found. Also, be aware that there may be copyright issues with this technique – some publishers may require you to purchase electronic indices or other database versions of the set rather than to find this sort of 'homebrew' solution, and some may even consider an index as 'intellectual property' rather than merely a finding aid. So find out.

Finally, consider that others may have already done this work for common sets, or that older editions (maybe even your editions) of many reference works may already be partially or fully scanned and viewable in Google Books or in the intranets of organizations you might ally yourself with. Why duplicate work efforts when libraries could share?

This project is a simple hack in theory, but clearly workflow issues and standardization of the documentation process will lead to complexities. Fortunately, these are exactly the kinds of complexities that librarians are good at working through and making simpler.

Music Swap Party

This one might get you in trouble, and if it does I'm not liable, and neither is my publisher. Set out half a dozen of your laptops around a table (or arrange your desktop computers around a social space, maybe a crescent or circular table, so that folks can talk). Create a big obvious file folder icon on the desktop of each machine. Each desktop will have a folder labeled with a genre name. Depending on what you know about the interests of your community, these may be: Grunge, Drum n' Bass, Alt-Country, Neo-Pscyhedelic Rock, Twentieth-Century Operas, Grime ... the possibilities are practically endless. These folders need not be full of music – you might just seed each with one or two songs typical of the genre (so the machine with Grime gets 'Fire Fire' by M.I.A. and an untitled free style B-side from Chipmunk).

The doors open. Welcome everybody and lay down the rules. The rules are:

1. This is a Music Swap Party – sorry, meant to say: this is a File Swap Party.

2. You can sit at a machine and upload or download files to and from your personal media device.

3. Leave or take whatever you want with the understanding that the library is not liable for you breaking any laws. We are not encouraging you to break laws. We are just providing you with the facilities for finding and sharing information. Keep it legal, keep it safe.

Something like that. Pump tunes from a random playlist of related music through good speakers (hit some of the music blog search and aggregator sites, like playlist.com). Provide food. Provide drinks. Talk to folks, circulate, ask questions, groove a little bit. Have fun.

You can make such a party as genre-specific as you feel as necessary (the flier reads: 'Thursday night, starting @ 6 pm, Library will host Music Swap Party for Side Projects and Solo Work of the members of Led Zeppelin! Zoso till the Lights Go OUT!), or leave it wide open: 'General Music Swap, Anything Goes.'

This program can be modified for educational or community-building purposes directed at clubs and organizations. You might host a Swap Party for songs created only with renaissance era instruments for the Society for Creative Anachronisms. Or a 'great speeches' swap of spoken word pieces for the History Book Club. You get the idea.

To help pave the way for this program's success, you will want to identify members of your community who can help lead this effort by talking to their peers about the program to drum up some interest ahead of time Also, if a few key volunteers share some of their own tracks from their own file collections to get things going (it would be a disappointment if, after all, people showed up with not enough music to swap, or if everyone who came already had the same songs – sorry, I mean files), it will 'prime the pump' for others to share their own.

Creative Commons workshop

This is good not just for your patrons, but also for your staff. Librarians and educators have a rather touchy history with copyright law – figuring out what counts as fair use and what crosses the line into copyright abuse is not always particularly easy for the non-lawyerly. One innovative initiative to help simplify intellectual property rights and usage is Creative Commons – in fact, it is a new way to think about copyright and intellectual property. Sometimes referred to as 'copyleft' due its more liberal (as in freedom-granting) stances toward usage rights, Creative Commons allows the creators or authors of works to granulate the rights of those using or wishing to modify the originals. This means that as the writer or artist or performer, you can unilaterally grant users the right to use your work in specific ways. This might range from the very open (remix freely, use commercially, no attribution required) to very restrictive (full copyright protection, all rights reserved).

Creative Commons does not answer all the important questions, though. It doesn't even come close, especially when we work with items that are restrictively copyrighted, but we know we do have certain rights as educators to reuse the material. What are the responsibilities of librarians in educating our community members about copyright law? The debate is long and fairly tedious. Carrie Russell's *Complete Copyright* (2004) is a thorough, informative, and very usable guide to copyright law for libraries, and may serve as a ready text to draw from for a program on these issues.

Beagle offers up the notion of a free-trade zone for copyright – a 'copyright-free zone' in which a network of information commons and library partners 'establish a "closed circuit network" operating in parallel to the normal open Internet infrastructure ... accessible from workstations and data points physically located in campus-based [information commons and learning centers],' with no commercial access to these network entry points (2006: 188).

Such workshops based on copyright, copyleft, intellectual property, and public domain would be of particular benefit to students as a way to teach, through real cases and object lessons, the importance of these issues as they relate to plagiarism and intellectual honesty.

References

AADL (Ann Arbor District Library) (2008) 'About Us.' Online at: *http://www.aadl.org/aboutus/*.

Alexander, L. (2008) 'World of Warcraft hits over 10 million subscribers,' *Gamasutra*. Online at: *http://www.gamasutra .com/php-bin/news_index.php?story=17062*.

Au, W.J. (2008) *The Making of Second Life: Notes from the New World*. New York: Collins.

Bauman, Z. (1998) *Globalization: The Human Consequences*. Cambridge: Polity Press.

Beagle, D. (2006) *The Information Commons Handbook*. New York: Neal-Schuman.

Benjamin, W. (1936) 'The Work of Art in the Age of Mechanical Reproduction.' Online at: *http://www.marxists .org/reference/subject/philosophy/works/ge/benjamin.htm*.

boyd, d. (2006) 'Facebook's "privacy trainwreck": exposure, invasion, and drama,' *Apophenia Blog*, 8 September. Online at: *http://www.danah.org/papers/FacebookAnd Privacy.html*.

Carr, N. (2008) 'Is Google making us stupid?' *Atlantic Monthly*. Online at: *http://www.theatlantic.com/doc/ 200807/google*.

Carse, J. (1987) *Finite and Infinite Games*. New York: Ballantine.

Castronova, E. (2005) *Synthetic Worlds*. Chicago: Chicago University Press.

Crowe, N. (2006) '"Hanging out in RuneScape": identity, work and leisure in the virtual playground,' *Children's Geographies*, 4(3): 331–46.

Dasgupta, K. (2000) *Libraries and Librarians in India on the Threshold of the 3rd Millennium: Challenges and Risks*. Paper presented at the 66th Annual International Federation of Library Associations and Institutions, Jerusalem. Online at: *http://www.ifla.org/IV/ifla66/papers/039-120e.htm*.

Dillon, A. (2000) 'Group dynamics meet cognition: combining socio-technical concepts and usability engineering in the design of information systems,' in E. Coakes et al. (eds), *The New Socio Tech: Graffiti on the Long Wall*. London: Springer-Verlag, pp. 119–26.

Elf (2008) *What Does Elf Do?* Jandi Enterprises. Online at: *http://www.libraryelf.com/FAQ.aspx*.

Elliot, M. (2002) 'Gossip Folks,' *Under Construction*. Elektra Records.

Ellis, W. (2007) 'Shipwrecked and abandoned,' *Second Life Sketches*. Thomson Reuters. Online at: *http://secondlife.reuters.com/stories/2007/05/11/second-life-sketches-shipwrecked-and-abandoned/*.

Evans, W. (2006) 'NextGen: they're RFIDs, not Arphids,' *Library Journal*, 15 November. Online at: *http://www.libraryjournal.com/article/CA6388327.html*.

Evans, W. (2007a) 'My MySpace comment,' *Library Journal*, 15 February. Online at: *http://www.libraryjournal.com/article/CA6413453.html*.

Evans, W. (2007b) 'We find it all: Wikia's new social search engine,' *Newsbreaks*. Information Today. Online at: *http://newsbreaks.infotoday.com/nbReader.asp?ArticleId=40606*.

Evans, W. (2008) 'Embryonic Web 3.0: universal search, Wikia, and the birth of user-generated search,' *Searcher*, 16(1): 12.

Evans, W. (2009) 'Searching the Widgetized Web,' *Searcher*, 17(1): 10.

Farkas, M. (2007) *Social Software in Libraries: Building Collaboration, Communication, and Community Online.* Medford, NJ: Information Today.

Fischetti, T. and Berners-Lee, T. (1999) *Weaving the Web: The Original Design and Ultimate Destiny of the World Wide Web.* New York: HarperCollins.

Fregoso, G. (2007) 'RFID in the United Kingdom,' in J. Banks et al. (eds), *RFID Applied.* Hoboken, NJ: Wiley, pp. 439–44.

Gershenfeld, N. (1999) *When Things Start to Think.* New York: Henry Holt.

Gibbons, S. (2007) *The Academic Library and the Net Gen Student.* Chicago: American Library Association.

Gorman, M. (1998) *Our Singular Strengths: Meditations for Librarians.* Chicago: American Library Association.

Greenfield, A. (2006) *Everyware: The Dawning Age of Ubiquitous Computing.* Berkeley, CA: New Riders.

Hani, Y. (2007) 'Cellphone bards hit bestseller lists,' *Japan Times Online.* 23 September. Online at: *http://search.japantimes.co.jp/cgi-bin/fl20070923x4.html.*

Hanson, J. (2007) *24/7.* Westport, CT: Praeger.

Hansmann, U. (2003) *Pervasive Computing.* New York: Springer-Verlag.

Harris, S. et al. (2005) *Gray Hat Hacking: The Ethical Hacker's Handbook.* New York: McGraw-Hill.

Herring, M. (2005) 'A gaggle of Googles,' in W. Miller et al. (eds), *Libraries and Google.* New York: Hawthorn Press, pp. 37–44.

Himanen, P. (2001) *The Hacker Ethic and the Spirit of the Information Age.* New York: Random House.

Humble, T. (2008) 'RFID Excerpt'. Personal communication.

Internet World Stats (2007) Online at: *http://www.internetworldstats.com/eu/uk.htm.*

IT Facts (2007) *http://www.itfacts.biz/500-mln-cell-phone-accounts-in-china/8549.*

Jardin, X. (2008) 'How to hack RFID-enabled credit cards for $8,' *BoingBoing TV*. Online at: *http://tv.boingboing.net/2008/03/19/how-to-hack-an-rfide.html.*

Kozierok, C.M. (2007) 'RuneScape exposed part 1: an education kids don't need,' *Tom's Games*. Best of Media Group. Online at: *http://www.tomsgames.com/us/2007/03/26/RuneScape_exposed/index.html.*

Kroski, E. (2007) 'Folksonomies and user-based tagging,' in N. Courtney (ed.), *Library 2.0 and Beyond*. Westport, CT: Libraries Unlimited, pp. 91–103.

Liu, S. (2007) 'Extended memory RFID tags provide immediate access to data anywhere, anytime,' White Paper, *Intelleflex*. Open Systems Publishing. Online at: *http://www.industrial-embedded.com/pdfs/Intelleflex.Win07.pdf.*

Ludlow, P. (2007) *The Second Life Herald: The Virtual Tabloid that Witnessed the Dawn of the Metaverse*. Cambridge, MA: MIT.

McGowan, A. (2007) *The Educational Benefits of Playing RuneScape*. Associated Content. Online at: *http://www.associatedcontent.com/article/124817/the_educational_benefits_of_playing.html.*

Meetup Note (2008) Meetup.com. Online at: *http://www.meetup.com/about/.*

Merk, L. et al. (2001) *Pervasive Computing Handbook*. Berlin: Springer-Verlag Telos.

Morville, P. (2005) *Ambient Findability*. Sebastopol, CA: O'Reilly.

Morville, P. et al. (2002) *Information Architecture for the World Wide Web: Designing Large-Scale Web Sites*. Sebastopol, CA: O'Reilly.

Nielsen, J. (1994) *Usability Engineering*. San Francisco: Morgan Kaufmann.

OCLC (2005) 'Perceptions of Libraries and Information Resources.' Online at: *http://www.oclc.org/us/en/reports/2005perceptions.htm*.

Onishi, N. (2008) 'Thumbs race as Japan's best sellers go cellular,' *New York Times*. Online at: *http://www.nytimes.com/2008/01/20/world/asia/20japan.html*.

O'Reilly, T. (2005) *What Is Web 2.0?* O'Reilly Media, Inc. Online at: *http://www.oreillynet.com/pub/a/oreilly/tim/news/2005/09/30/what-is-web-20.html*.

Peters, T. (2007) *A Report on the First Year of Operation of the Alliance Second Life Library 2.0 Project*. Alliance Library System. Online at: *http://www.alliancelibrarysystem.com/pdf/07sllreport.pdf*.

Pew Research Center (2005) 'Pew Internet & American Life Project.' Online at: *http://www.pewinternet.org/*.

Phillips, A. (2006) 'RuneScape,' *School Library Journal*, 52(10): 81.

Rosenberg, R. (2004) *The Social Impact of Computers*. London: Elsevier.

Rushkoff, D. (1999) *Coercion: Why We Listen to What 'They' Say*. New York: Riverhead.

Rushkoff, D. (2002) *Exit Strategy*. New York: Soft Skull Press.

Russell, C. (2004) *Complete Copyright: An Everyday Guide for Librarians*. Chicago: American Library Association.

Sheila Greco Associates, LLC (2008) *SGA Executive Tracker*. Linden Research. Online at: *http://www.sgaexecutivetracker.com/*.

Silberglitt, R. et al. (2006) *The Global Technology Revolution 2020, In-Depth Analyses Bio/Nano/Materials/Information Trends, Drivers, Barriers, and Social Implications*. Rand Corporation, National Security Research Division. Online at: *http://www.rand.org/pubs/technical_reports/2006/RAND_TR303.pdf*.

Smith, S. (2008) Comment at 'Second Life Library Quick Note'. ISHUSH. Online at: *http://ishush.blogspot.com/2008/06/second-life-library-quick-note.html*.

Stack, L. (2008) 'Politics on Facebook brings trouble for young Egpytian,' *Christian Science Monitor*, 7 July. Online at: *http://features.csmonitor.com/innovation/2008/07/07/politics-on-facebook-brings-trouble-for-young-egyptian/*.

Sterling, B. (2005) *Shaping Things*. Cambridge, MA: MIT Press.

Tennant, R. (2007) 'Will RDA be DOA?' *Library Journal*, 15 March. Online at: *http://www.libraryjournal.com/article/CA6422278.html*.

Textually (2006) 'Up to 90 percent of globe to have mobile coverage.' Online at: *http://www.textually.org/textually/archives/2006/10/013841.htm*.

Wilson, R.A. (2007) *Ghostfooting*. Online at: *http://ghostfeet.wordpress.com/2007/07/23/gaming-culture-libraries/*.

Wolf, C. (2006) *Basic Library Skills*. Jefferson, NC: McFarland.

World Wide Web Consortium (W3C) (2004) 'RDF Primer.' Online at: *http://www.w3.org/TR/REC-rdf-syntax/*.

Wright, A. (2007) *Glut: Mastering Information Through the Ages*. Washington, DC: Joseph Henry Press.

Index